SIMPLIFY

—— YOUR ——

RETIREMENT

SIMPLIFY

--- YOUR ---

RETIREMENT

TIMELESS PRINCIPLES TO ACHIEVE

FINANCIAL PEACE

STEPHEN STRICKLIN, CFP®, CKA®

Published by Advantage, Charleston, South Carolina.
Member of Advantage Media Group.

ADVANTAGE is a registered trademark, and the Advantage colophon is a trademark of Advantage Media Group, Inc.

Printed in the United States of America.

10 9 8 7 6 5 4 3 2 1

ISBN: 978-1-59932-818-8
LCCN: 2017937242

Cover design by Katie Biondo.

This publication is designed to provide accurate and authoritative information in regard to the subject matter covered. It is sold with the understanding that the publisher is not engaged in rendering legal, accounting, or other professional services. If legal advice or other expert assistance is required, the services of a competent professional person should be sought.

Advantage Media Group is proud to be a part of the Tree Neutral® program. Tree Neutral offsets the number of trees consumed in the production and printing of this book by taking proactive steps such as planting trees in direct proportion to the number of trees used to print books. To learn more about Tree Neutral, please visit **www.treeneutral.com**.

Advantage Media Group is a publisher of business, self-improvement, and professional development books. We help entrepreneurs, business leaders, and professionals share their Stories, Passion, and Knowledge to help others Learn & Grow. Do you have a manuscript or book idea that you would like us to consider for publishing? Please visit **advantagefamily.com** or call **1.866.775.1696.**

TABLE OF CONTENTS

ACKNOWLEDGMENTS

To my sweet wife, Amy, and to our four children, Andrew, Emma, Seth, and Kate, for your patience and love.

To my loving parents, family, former employers, teachers, and coaches, for all that you taught me about life, work, and service.

To Paul Brock and the team at Wise Wealth, LLC, for helping me write this book and developing an investment firm that lives out the Golden Rule.

To my clients, for your trust and loyalty.

To God be the glory.

Financial Planning as a Calling

E ach of us reaches a crossroads in life, sometimes several, and a major one for me came a few years after I left my native Rhode Island to attend seminary in Kansas City. As I was trying to figure out what God wanted to do with my life, I could finally see how it was all coming together in his perfect timing.

I grew up in church. My father was a Baptist pastor in Rhode Island, and he started a Christian school. Not only did I attend that school, I also went to a private Christian college—and when I graduated, it was back to Rhode Island to join my dad's church staff and to teach and coach at the school. A year later, I married Amy, whom I had met at the college in my sophomore year.

Life was comfortable and enjoyable for those six years, and I treasure that time and the relationships I developed. I am a teacher at heart, and those experiences shaped me. I found fulfillment in motivating others to do their best, individually and as part of a team. It was the foundation for my career today as a financial advisor. At the time, however, I was restless, and I increasingly felt the need to figure out what God's purpose or calling was for me personally.

When we left Rhode Island for Kansas City in 2003, I imagined myself in full-time ministry, perhaps starting a church in Boston. I felt confident that my calling was to get my master's degree in theology and become a pastor like my father before me. The plan was to finish seminary in two years. Meanwhile, our family was growing. Amy and I already had a little boy, and a month after moving to Kansas City, she gave birth to a girl. Today, after eighteen years of marriage, we are the proud parents of two boys and two girls.

The seminary expected students to become involved in the community, holding a daytime job and attending classes at night and on weekends. I took a job with the teacher-insurance company, Horace Mann—it seemed a good fit for me because I had been a teacher and had long been interested in money matters. I had a paper route when I was a boy, and my father encouraged my four brothers and me to handle money wisely. I had read books and watched videos by Larry Burkett (of Crown Financial Ministries) and Bruce Wilkinson (out of Dallas Theological Seminary). During the roaring '90s, I tried my hand at investing and became fascinated with the potential of the markets, although I learned some hard lessons about the danger of market timing and of chasing returns.

Though I did not yet feel that a position in the financial industry was my calling, it did seem an intriguing endeavor while I was at seminary. I continued to pray for God's direction. One day, my younger brother Timothy told me about a guy he had been listening to on the radio in Tennessee by the name of Dave Ramsey—who would become nationally known as a leader in personal financial management. I quickly found and purchased his newly published book, *The Total Money Makeover*. The book spoke to my life. I was a seminary student with a young family, and we were struggling with practical financial management. We found ourselves in debt, and I particularly needed wisdom and direction for our family finances.

This was a wake-up call. How could I expect to go into ministry unless I could handle money well myself? After a year in seminary, I felt that getting my own personal finances under control needed to be the priority. And I felt something else. As I read the Ramsey book, I began to feel that the financial industry was *my calling*. This was what God had for me. I became very passionate about that prospect. I studied everything I could find in the Bible about money and finances—and I discovered that Jesus had more to say about financial management than he did about almost any other single topic. Clearly, financial stewardship was a divine priority.

I decided that I would step away from my seminary studies while Amy and I endeavored to get out of debt and get our own financial house in order—and that is what we worked to do for the next two years. I felt that I needed to have a solid financial foundation before I made a career of helping others with their finances. After getting my insurance licenses at Horace Mann, I left to take a job with AG Edwards, where I got my securities licenses and learned much about the investment world. During our third year in Kansas City, I switched to a job with Pioneer Financial Services, where I led the internal sales of corporate notes.

I also enrolled in the University of Missouri-Kansas City Financial Planning Certificate Program. All the while, I was studying what the Bible had to say about money and finances as well, and I became increasingly confident that God had revealed his calling for me. And so, in our fourth year in Kansas City, I returned to seminary to finish the program, getting my master's in theology in 2007. And six months later, I passed the exams and met the stringent requirements to become a CERTIFIED FINANCIAL PLANNER™ practitioner.

A DOOR CLOSED, A CALLING FULFILLED

It was clear to me by then that I needed to take a different path in the financial industry. In 2006, my position at Pioneer Financial was eliminated in a buyout, but I got a severance package—which was quite remarkable, since I had not been there long. Pioneer, in essence, was offering to continue to pay me while also encouraging me to move on to the next phase of my career.

All right, God, my heart whispered, *this is it, isn't it?* It was clear to me that he did not want me to just move on to work at some big broker-dealer. He wanted me to take what I had learned in the industry and transform it into an enterprise that would be true to myself and my beliefs and that would reflect his will. This created an opportunity for me to take what I had learned up to this point in the financial-services industry—both positive and negative—along with a passion to help others succeed, in order to open a new firm based on timeless principles with education and planning as a foundation for everything else.

The financial package I received from my job position being eliminated was what gave me the freedom to transition my life and the life of my family. This was the incentive and the catalyst to start my business and fulfill my calling. God was giving me this opportunity. I would either make it or I would stumble. I launched Wise Wealth in February 2007, and this year we are celebrating our tenth anniversary. Through God's grace, I have made it this far.

I named my firm Wise Wealth for two reasons. My studies of biblical financial principles had led me to Proverbs 24:3–4, which says: "Through wisdom is a house built, and by understanding it is established, and by knowledge shall the rooms be filled with pleasant and precious riches." In other words: *First Wisdom, Then Wealth.* It's become the slogan of my business. I had already seen many people trying to build wealth without having a plan. They did not really know why they owned what they owned. They had an assortment of investment holdings that did not fit together and certainly did not have a plan. Wisdom requires a plan first.

Up to that point, all my "formal training" in the financial industry had been straight to the money. It was about sales and pushing products, regardless of the clients' needs. We were told how and what to sell. I had come to understand that a financial plan must be more than what you own. It must embrace why you own it. How does it fit in your life? Financial planning is about attaining financial peace—which does not come from products or portfolios—but rather from a strategy built around your values and goals.

That biblical principle of wisdom before wealth is the cornerstone of my business today. It is a universal and timeless approach that I take as I work with people of any religion or creed. I seek first to understand my clients' goals and values and the end results that they seek. Only then can I make the proper recommendations on the investments.

I felt that it was important that my business be independent and not beholden to any insurance or investment company. That way I could be true to my beliefs and to my clients' interests, not to some parent company's requirements. I wanted to be full service so that I could offer whatever products were appropriate and necessary to serve those interests. I wished to function as a true fiduciary.

As I was preparing to open my business, I thought about how influential the Dave Ramsey book had been for me. I took the time to go through his certified counselor training course. Also pivotal in my life at that time was Ron Blue's Kingdom Advisors organization, which offers training and support to financial professionals who want to integrate their Christian faith with their practice. It was reassuring to know that others also viewed financial planning as a calling. Like them, I could see my chosen profession as a ministry.

STEPS TOWARD A VISION

My goal from the start had been to build a business to the point where I would be able to support my family by working Monday through Thursday so that on weekends I could volunteer in churches to teach financial management from a biblical perspective. With the heart of a teacher and a passion to make an impact, God has helped me to attain the desires of my heart. I developed and teach a course called "Simplify Your Retirement" for use with anyone at or near retirement, and I have also designed another called "Managing God's Resources" for use in churches or Christian organizations.

This book is another step in that vision. It is built upon the faith that inspires and defines me, but I am not presuming that all my readers will share that faith. I do intend to write another book designed specifically for pastors and ministers and other Christian believers, but this one is for anyone interested in the fundamental truths of retirement and financial planning. I wish to reach out to all people who want to manage their wealth wisely.

It is my privilege to share with you some practical wisdom in this book. As a teacher and a coach, I strive to make things clear. Financial salespeople and the media can make it all seem so complex as they urge you to buy and sell or to get in and get out. My kind of motivation is based on simplicity. A financial plan need not be extremely complex. I try to put it on one page if possible. Once we get it to its essence, it becomes the blueprint for adding as many details as necessary.

Retirement planning really amounts to following some essential rules and using the appropriate tools to build toward your objectives—anticipating and dealing with anything that might threaten your ability to reach them. You cannot and should not just throw your money into the market and hope for the best. This book will address a better, more principled and purposeful way to allocate your assets for retirement.

Whatever your goals in life might be, certainly a sense of security is one of them. In this book, I will help you cut through the clutter to give you clarity about the governing principles behind effective retirement planning. I will share time-tested wisdom with you and show you how to craft a plan based on that wisdom so that you and your family can pursue your dreams with financial peace of mind.

INTRODUCTION

A Principled Approach

I have long noticed a trend among those who become my clients. They tend to have done a good job of accumulating and saving money. They feel that they "probably" have enough to retire, although they want some reassurance. They have seen how people can lose much of their savings quite easily, and so they put their money in very safe investments—but they also know that it should not just be sitting there earning nothing.

That is where many of my top clients were when they came to me. They had saved a lot of money, but they did not know whether they should be in the market or on the sidelines. They knew they needed to be doing something—but what? Not knowing left them feeling paralyzed.

I quickly help them to gain clarity. First, we determine how much liquid money they need for an emergency fund and for any known purchases or expenses in the next three to five years. Next, we come to terms with the income number: How much money will they need each month—not just to pay the bills but also to support their desired lifestyle? We help them see how much of their current assets will be needed to cover their income needs. And then, after taking care of those liquidity and income needs, they can set aside whatever money remains for growth. That's how much money they can reasonably put at risk in the market.

After that, there is no more guessing. They have the answer to their question. They know how much should be in the bank and how much should be in the market. The latter amount will not affect their income and lifestyle. My philosophy is that my clients should *protect their income* and liquidity first so that they will not be worried about that throughout retirement. The rest they can put at risk for the potential of greater gain.

As a financial planner who helps people prepare for retirement, I have often seen two types of fear. Many people are scared of losing their money if they invest it in the market, and at the same time they worry that they won't gain enough if they just leave it in the bank. I'm sure that describes many of you who are reading this book. You want peace of mind, but you don't know how to get it.

YOU COME FIRST

Will you have enough money to retire? Even the affluent ask themselves that. They want to maintain their accustomed lifestyle for the rest of their years and perhaps leave a legacy for their loved ones. In the approach to retirement, *the focus must shift from accumulating money to preserving and protecting it so that it can be distributed for a lifelong income.*

Many people do not effectively make that switch. They do not adjust to the new rules—because nobody has told him that they must do so. They may have done well in life, but their expertise is in something other than financial planning, and they have never developed a relationship with the kind of planner who will be firmly on their side. Some advisors will tell them to leave all their money in the market, and some will implore them to play it safe with every cent. Prospective retirees, even if they know that neither extreme is wise, generally do not know where or how to strike the balance.

At this stage of life, you cannot afford to get it wrong. When you were in your thirties and forties, you could make mistakes in your investing and in your asset allocation and still have time to recover. Now, you lack that time, and you cannot afford those mistakes. *Generally, the industry helps people effectively accumulate money, but you need a different type of assistance when it comes time to preserve your money and draw an income from it.*

It is more essential than ever that your investments fit your purpose. An advisor who has only one solution is *not* the one for you. You need an impartial specialist who understands and has had extensive experience with the issues of retirement—and you must be confident that person serves only your specific interests and not those of some corporate board.

You come first. Not only must your advisor be solely on your side but he or she must take the time to get to know you before getting into the specifics of investments and the wide range of products that may or may not be in your best interest. There will be a time to dig into the accounts and the amounts later, but the first part of the process is all about you and your story. What are your goals in life? What are your retirement dreams made of? Is your money being managed in a way that improves your life? The advisor who sincerely wants to know that about you is the advisor who will treat you right and direct your path wisely.

IS THIS BOOK FOR YOU?

You will be glad to know that unlike many other financial advisors who require a minimum of $500,000 or more before you can request their help, the principles found in this book work for anyone, regardless of the size of their investment portfolio. My typical client is five to ten years from retiring or perhaps in the beginning stages of retirement. Younger people certainly need a financial plan as well, but while they are in the accumulation phase, they are more likely to be focusing on growth. For most of my clients, the focus is more on preservation and on producing a retirement income.

Many of my clients are small-business owners and executives. I also work with doctors and dentists and other individuals who have been good savers during their careers. They have attained a relatively high net worth, and they have reached the point where they are concerned about what might become of their money if they do not properly manage it. They have become increasingly aware that they no longer have the luxury of youthful mistakes in their financial decisions. They have recognized that they need a plan, and they want clarity and freedom from worries. They tend to adopt the philosophy of Will Rogers, who said, "People should be more concerned with the return *of* their principal than the return *on* their principal."

In this book, I reach out primarily to pre-retirees and retirees who are in those critical years of fifty to seventy. For the most part, they are done with the accumulation stage of life and are eager to know what comes next and what they need to do. This involves much more than just plain old investment advice. Retirement planning includes a broad range of services, all of which must work together. If someone were to walk into my office and seem to want only some hot investment tip, I strongly doubt we would be a good fit. How could I know what would be best for that person, when we had done little more than shake hands?

This book is for people who want to see their investments grow—but only that portion of their money that they can afford to have at risk. This book is for people who understand that they must know *why* they are investing and who want to clarify their purpose and goals in life. Before risking anything, they need to make sure they have covered their short-term needs and that they have secured a lifelong income.

Also, unlike many advisors, I do not give investment recommendations outside the context of a plan, and we cannot create that plan simply from your answers to a risk profile questionnaire. Instead, I will take the time and ask about the purpose of the money—whether it is for current income, for example, or for some future goal—and the extent to which it needs to be accessible. Is the objective safety? Or income? Or growth?

It is the overall financial plan that will determine the products and investments that will make the most sense. My clients understand that, and they know that the comprehensive approach that they get from me is not something they could hope to attain from some online robo-advisor or, frankly, from most people in the financial industry. I treat my clients as more than just a number, more than just a risk-profile score, more than just an asset-allocation problem to be solved. I write this book for those who are interested in a *relationship*.

FIVE PRINCIPLES OF FINANCIAL PLANNING

Let's review the five principles of financial planning that characterize my approach and that you will find woven throughout the chapters of this book. These principles have been born out of years of experience and observation about what works and what does not work. The essence of my approach is that wisdom comes first. If you do not have a philosophy, then you are more likely to be swayed the wrong way by what you see on TV or hear on the radio or read in a magazine article. You will feel tempted to try one thing today, another tomorrow—and unless you have a purpose behind your investments, you will feel frustrated and unclear about whether you are doing the right thing. Sound familiar?

1.   No investment decisions outside the context of the plan.

"So what do you think about gold?" people sometimes ask. "What do you think about annuities?" The questions take many forms, but my answer is consistent: "It depends." There is no such thing as a bad investment. There is just a bad fit.

There is a place for almost every investment, and every investment can be put into places where it should not be. Proper investment placement will depend in large part upon the context of your financial plan. Does the investment fit your need for liquidity? For income? For growth? What are the specific risks that you are facing, and how would that investment help you, or hinder you, in that regard?

The investment needs to function in a specific way within your plan to advance your goals for retirement. If it does not do that, it is not a good investment for you. If it does, then you are on the right track. We cannot know one way or the other, however, outside the context of your plan. A specific investment may be a great fit for your neighbor or your uncle or your coworker, but it might be a terrible one for you.

2. The plan determines the products.

Generally speaking, there are three types of products: bank products, brokerage products, and insurance products. How are you going to know the right combination for your portfolio and how to put each of those options to their best use?

People are often sold various investments that might sound good in an advertisement but that don't fit well into their plan. They turn their attention to certificates of deposit, fixed annuities, mutual funds, or whatever is on their mind, depending upon the latest snippet of information they got from one source or another. Any of those might be a good choice, and any of those could be a big mistake.

If you need relatively safe and accessible money, some products are designed to provide it and others will never function that way. If you want growth, some products will undoubtedly disappoint you, while others may provide much greater potential to increase your returns. If you want guaranteed income, you must choose the products designed for that purpose. The right investments and products will depend upon what you need and want, as you have set forth in your plan.

3. Don't let your portfolio take a H.I.T.

Three of the biggest risks that retirees need to address in their financial plan are *health care*, *inflation*, and *taxes*. You do not have a plan unless you have addressed those "big three." What are the potential financial risks that you will be facing for medical care and possibly long-term custodial care? Inflation, too, must be specifically addressed. We must make sure that the ever-increasing cost of living will not begin to erode the quality of your lifestyle, and so your portfolio must grow sufficiently to keep pace. And we must also account for taxes, another hard-to-predict variable.

The extent of the hit from H.I.T. is hard to gauge, but it must not be taken lightly. These three will certainly make an impact, and their effect on your portfolio must be anticipated and incorporated in your financial plan. You must not leave it all up to chance.

4.   Protect the income; grow the rest.

Many people are afraid that they will outlive their assets and run out of money. Few have pensions anymore, and their Social Security benefits are insufficient. They need to produce most of their income from the investment power of the assets that they have accumulated.

That ability to produce income must not be exposed to risk. Some clients want to use a guaranteed product to insure their income, and so we may use an annuity to cover their living expenses so that they do not have to worry about whether they will outlive their money. They will get a regular paycheck for life. Others may not want to buy an annuity, but they would need to be extremely conservative in how they invest the portion of their portfolio that they had set aside to produce income.

You must safeguard the amount of your savings that is necessary to produce your desired income. After you have done so, you can afford to take a risk with whatever is left. In fact, you may find that the reassurance that you have gained from securing your income will give you the freedom to invest more aggressively for growth. That is because you can now proceed with confidence, unhindered by fear.

5. Financial peace comes from having a plan.

Your financial plan is what gives you the opportunity for financial peace. No product can provide that for you. No asset-allocation model can provide that for you. It is not a feeling that arises as you answer questions from a risk profile. Financial peace comes from knowing that you have anticipated and done your best to manage all the risks that you could face. It comes from knowing that you will have enough money to meet all your needs and your desired lifestyle throughout retirement. It comes from knowing that you will have sufficient money ready and waiting for all of life's contingencies.

When I meet with clients for annual reviews, certainly we talk about investment performance and all the many details. Those do matter—but they are not what is most important. Yes, we can look at whether one fund is better than another, but what matters most is whether my clients have attained confidence that all is well. What we are really determining is your "return on life," not just your "return on investment." Is the plan allowing you to live your life the way that you want to?

What I want to know is whether they are staying true to the plan. Is it meeting their needs and objectives? I want my clients to feel confident regardless of what is happening on the political and economic scene in the nation and the world. I want them to feel the security of having a reliable plan in place even when the unexpected comes their way. In other words, I want my clients to receive the true dividends of a principled approach to financial planning—financial peace of mind.

CHAPTER 1

Phases of Investing

Anyone who has given much thought to preparing for retirement has probably come across some of the "rules" that are often espoused as essential guidelines for success: the Rule of 100, for example, the 4 percent withdrawal rule, or the 80 percent cost-of-living rule, etc. The trouble with these rules is that they attempt to apply generic advice to people whose lives differ in a variety of ways. This is the same issue with retirement planning as it typically is conducted: it tries to cram people into boxes. It tries to fit one person's retirement plan into somebody else's idea of what is suitable. It ignores the fact that individuals and couples and families each are unique, with differing goals and dreams. It ignores what should be obvious: retirement is a new phase of life, with new challenges and risks, that calls for a customized approach.

Financial security depends upon a period of comprehensive planning that addresses each of the risks that could potentially derail your retirement. A stock-market crash might come to mind first, but those threats also could include expenses related to illness, family emergencies, tax matters, inflation, and the death or incapacitation of a spouse. More than ever, as couples struggle with life's tensions, the prospect of divorce also looms, highlighting the need to prepare emotionally as well as financially.

Here is a rule that should rise above any of the others: *The best measure of retirement success is your peace of mind.* How you define it will differ from how your neighbor or coworker or cousin defines it. For many, that peace is elusive because many people put off important decisions. That is no way to live. The time has come to set your sights on a clear destination and chart your course to get there. In doing so, peace of mind is what you will find along the way.

In this book, I will show you a far better way, and it is one that calls for a whole new mind-set. Once you understand that, you will be able to have a plan that makes sense for you and your family—a plan that will give you the life you want and that will support your dreams. You are entering new territory in retirement. Let's get ready.

EXCITING AND SCARY

The realities of retirement catch many people by surprise. They may have harbored some idyllic image of how life would be. Some imagine rest and leisure. Others look forward to pursuing long-delayed delights. Some expect to lay back and some expect to give back. Often this is a time for new endeavors, such as traveling and volunteering. Some may begin a new career. All of that is fine, of course, so long as it is by choice. You should not be retiring before you are ready, and you should not *have* to return to work to survive.

One client told me that all he wanted to do was "sit on the porch and watch the grass grow," while another couple told me of their desire to "buy a fifth-wheel or RV and tour the country." Some have wanted to take the whole family on a trip to Disney World and still others have expressed a desire to live somewhere warm.

People's retirement expectations often have much to do with what they observed in previous generations. The world has picked up its pace, however, and retirement lasts much longer than was once the case. In 1970, the typical life expectancy for a man was about sixty-seven and for a woman was about seventy-five. The Census Bureau predicts that life expectancy will rise to seventy-seven for men and eighty-two for women by 2020.[1] One spouse or the other easily could live three decades or longer into retirement. Recent projections put the odds at about even that for a couple aged sixty-five, one spouse will live to ninety. Think about it—possibly three decades in retirement! Some people will need their savings to last just as long as they spent saving it to begin with. Your savings from age thirty-five to sixty-five may now have to pay you from age sixty-five to ninety-five.

That longevity offers new opportunities in life, of course, but it clearly presents new challenges as well. Aging bodies require more care and upkeep, with clear implications for rising medical costs. Financial tensions will mount as additional years of life and spending put further pressure on portfolios—particularly in an era when pensions are fading away and Social Security seems insecure. A longer retirement also means that inflation has more time to chip away at spending power. Inflation hits retirees particularly hard because of their greater demand for medical services, which in most recent years have significantly outpaced the overall inflation rate.

Instead of travel and relaxation, many people will find retirement to be a time of fear and uncertainty—unless they take purposeful action. The new retiree must face the reality that he or she will not be returning to work on Monday. Those regular paychecks from the employer that have come in for decades will cease, and that can feel

---

1   U.S. Census Bureau, Statistical Abstract of the United States, 2012, https://www.census.gov/prod/2011pubs/12statab/vitstat.pdf.

intimidating. Will there be a dependable cash flow to replace those checks?

The challenges are not just financial. This is also a time of social and emotional adjustment. Retirement can be the best years of life, but like any major change it can also be troubling. When the retirement parties are over, it is more than those paychecks that you will not be seeing anymore. It is unlikely that you will be seeing as much of your friends and associates from the workplace. They will move on, and you must too. Many people derive much of their personal identity from their career. What will replace that sense of contribution and belonging?

In short, what will you be doing now with all those additional hours of time? That is something that you need to consider every bit as much as the inner workings of your portfolio. What about the inner workings of your heart and mind? Have you prepared yourself for this upheaval in your routine? Most people are not happy, at least for long, sitting at home doing nothing. They often find that their spouses are not particularly pleased about that either!

I have seen what boredom does to people. They grow old more quickly, and their health suffers. They may become depressed in retirement, feeling as if they no longer matter. That feeling can be particularly acute among those who were executives and leaders in their careers. Once, entire staffs looked up to them, sought their opinions, listened to their decisions and directives; now, they may feel irrelevant.

The prospect of retirement is both exciting and scary. The key to finding success, in all things, is to plan appropriately and be prepared for whatever might come: financially, physically, spiritually, and emotionally.

A NEW PERSPECTIVE ON TIME

When you are contemplating retirement, life in many ways is much different than it was in your earlier days. Back then, it is likely that you focused on advancing in your career and raising a family, and you began to think about setting money aside for your children's college expenses. You may have bought a house and taken on an increasing load of debt that you worked for years to pay down. You were in building mode. It seemed to you then that your retirement was forever and a day away, but if you were wise you began to set money aside, accumulating what you could for some future undefined reality.

Your biggest asset in those days was time itself. With years stretching before you, you could afford more aggressive investments. You could take more risk, with the potential for more growth, because you would have time to rebuild if your investments didn't work out. If you took a loss, you could just try to earn more and keep adding to your investments, buying them at a bargain while you waited for the markets to recover—and you felt reasonably confident that all would be well.

Now, time isn't working on your side. Your portfolio very well might not be able to recover now if you make a mistake, or if the markets take a dive. You are becoming aware that *what you have accumulated is what must see you through.* You probably will not be adding to your nest egg as much anymore—if at all—and that is likely to make you feel more protective of it.

Your worries now are much different than those that preoccupied your younger self. Will you run out of money in retirement? Will the stock market deliver an unpleasant surprise? Will you be paying more than necessary in taxes? Will you be able to keep up with inflation? And what about your health? Will medical costs infringe on your lifestyle? What if you or your spouse need long-term care? These are among the biggest questions facing retirees. During the earning years, the biggest risk to a family is the possibility that the breadwinner could die early or become disabled. In retirement, the big financial risk is that life will linger for years while requiring some form of long-term care.

When you are sixty-five, the cares of life are every bit as consuming as they were when you were thirty-five. They are just different ones. As you can see, this new mind-set involves an array of concerns, and in one way or another they are related to the passage of time. Your outlook has matured. The planting and growing seasons are practically over, and now you are thinking more about reaping the harvest while protecting the storehouse.

A PARADIGM SHIFT

In this new season of life, the financial emphasis changes. As retirement approaches, fewer years remain in which you will be setting aside some of your paycheck to build your life savings. The emphasis now should switch to preserving what you have gathered because in a few short years you will be tapping into that money for a retirement income. Unless you come to terms with that truth and adjust your financial strategies, big trouble could lie ahead. The approach that you used throughout your accumulation years is likely to be counterproductive now.

Many financial planners speak in terms of two stages of financial life—accumulation and distribution. That model fails to recognize an essential intermediate step—the stage of preservation. You must have a transition time between growth mode and income-producing mode.

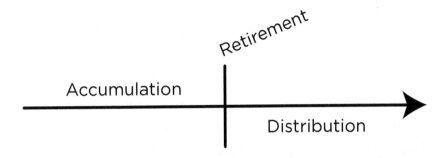

It is not easy to transition to the new mind-set. This is a paradigm shift. For decades you focused on accumulation and your investment goal was to take on as much risk as possible to get the highest-possible returns. Asset allocation was the most important aspect of investing in all the years leading up to retirement. Now I am saying that you have to switch gears from an investment mind-set that has allowed you to get to this moment. Oddly enough, *the strategy that got you here may not be what gets you through.* See, during the accumulation years when there were massive downward swings in the market, you had time to recover and you were still contributing during those times, which allowed you to buy low. But when you get within five to ten years of retirement, your portfolio may not have time to recover from a massive stock-market sell-off, and there is no way of knowing if that downtown will happen the very year you were planning to retire. We all have heard the stories of people whose retirement plans were delayed because they made no changes to their investment mind-set or allocations prior to retirement. Also, while you are drawing income from your investments in retirement, if the stock market were to drop by 20 percent while you are also withdrawing funds, it too can have a dramatic impact.

Many prospective retirees realize that they need to adjust, but they do little more than tinker with their asset allocations. Somewhere along the way they have heard the oft-touted Rule of 100. In short, that rule, which was set forth by Vanguard Group founder Jack Bogle, suggests that your investment mix be suitable for your age. Subtract your age from one hundred, the rule says, and the resulting number is the percentage of your portfolio to invest at risk in the stock market; the remainder should be invested more conservatively, which may be interpreted as bonds. As you get older, therefore, the mix supposedly becomes increasingly oriented toward financial security. The problem with that approach is that it does not really change anything except for your relative exposure to stocks and bonds. An asset-allocation model alone does not amount to retirement planning.

As some people approach retirement, they want to hold fast to their established patterns. They continue to tell themselves, for example, that over the years they have averaged a certain rate of return in the stock market and that the market always rebounds when it falls. They have been all right so far, they figure, and so they will be all right in retirement, too. What they do not understand is the importance of the sequence of those returns. In retirement, what matters is not the average rate of return but the real rate of return. If you take a big hit early in retirement while continuing to tap your portfolio for income, you may never recover. We will take a closer look at the principle of *sequence of returns* in chapter 4.

You cannot feel secure when all your investments are at the mercy of the markets. You need to know that you have sufficient funds to cover emergency expenses and that you have at least three to five years of known purchases and expenses kept safe despite whatever happens in the economy. You also need to protect your income. These involve solid projections, not guesses.

Another rule of thumb that often misleads people is the notion that they can withdraw 4 percent annually from their portfolio, no matter what, and never run out of money because the markets will accommodate that amount. Holding on to that mind-set, they go directly from the accumulation years to the distribution years. They see no reason to adjust their portfolio mix. They will just begin their 4 percent withdrawals and trust in market performance. They think that as long as their investments "average 6 percent per year and they withdraw no more than 4 percent per year that they can never run out of money." This is a false assumption. This strategy would definitely work if this was a fixed-rate investment, but since the markets are variable, the sequence of the returns becomes the key factor in whether or not a 4 percent withdrawal rate is sustainable.

The paradigm shift for retirement, in short, is that the focus changes from asset allocation to allocation based on priorities and purpose. The emphasis now must be on what you hope to accomplish with your money—which will determine how to invest it.

It's no longer as easy as it was in the accumulation years, when you could just aim for a percentage of growth or answer a risk profile (like an online robot might suggest). Young people often set aside money having little idea whether it will be sufficient for retirement, which underscores the fact that they, too, need a financial plan. They need a rate of return that will make retirement possible. In retirement, however, the focus is no longer on the investment return but instead on whether your investments are meeting their purposes. Your benchmark now is whether your financial plan is leading you to your life goals and giving you financial peace of mind.

WHEN TO START THE PRESERVATION PHASE

When you understand the importance of transitioning into a mind-set of *preservation before distribution,* you will want to make sure that you are working in the right time frame. My recommendation is that this phase be introduced five to ten years before your projected retirement date (or distribution phase).

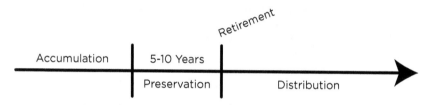

Five years is reasonable. For one thing, many people have a 401(k) or similar qualified plan and will face a penalty if they withdraw from it before they are 59½ years old. That, of course, limits their options for investing outside of the plan until they are within that five-year window.

In addition, five years or more is sufficient time for a well-diversified portfolio with a good asset allocation model to recover from any sort of market downturn. It is when you have less than five years that you need to pay particular attention to protecting your life savings from too much exposure to market risk. If you get too close to retirement before you adopt the preservation mind-set, you are at greater risk of having much less to preserve.

Although five years makes sense for those reasons, I sometimes recommend switching to preservation mode a decade before retirement, if at that point you already have sufficient assets to meet your projected income needs or if there is a guaranteed rate of return that will get you there. In that case, the time is ripe to preserve the appropriate amount until you need to draw that income. Anything beyond that amount, you can leave invested for continued growth. If you do not yet have the necessary resources to meet your retirement needs, however, you should be careful not to begin your preservation years prematurely.

UNIQUE BUT NOT ALONE

Although you are unique, I have seen some common themes among those who walk through my office door. I have heard the questions that so many people ask when they are contemplating retirement. The details differ, often dramatically, but they worry about the same sort of things. You are not alone.

Just as you need to make the paradigm shift from a mind-set of accumulation to one of preservation and then distribution, you also need to shift your thinking regarding financial advice. The kind that you have been getting all along may no longer serve you very well in the years ahead. That does not mean that you have had a bad financial advisor. That person (or online robot) was likely oriented toward accumulation, which was your focus at the time. That is not your focus now.

Instead, you should be working with a specialist in retirement-income planning (a real human being) who has the experience and expertise to help you sort through the many issues involved in designing a retirement plan that meets your needs. You need a *relationship* with someone who understands the risks and challenges of this stage of life and who has the solutions available to meet them. You only retire once, so you need the perspective of a planner who helps people retire every day. You have made it this far. You want to be in good hands the rest of the way. I will address what to look for in choosing a financial advisor in chapter 8.

CHAPTER 2

A New Retirement Reality

"One day you will understand," many of us recall our parents telling us when we were young, and eventually we came to appreciate their wisdom. It helped to see us through many of life's challenges. But when it comes to planning for retirement, what we need to understand is that what worked in the past often doesn't work anymore.

Previous generations relied on what often is described as the "three-legged stool" of retirement planning. They had the company pension, their Social Security benefit, and whatever savings they managed to set aside along the way. The Social Security leg of that stool has been getting weaker for years, and for many, the pension leg has fallen completely off. That leaves people more dependent than ever upon their own resources if they are to enjoy the standard of living that they expect.

The nature of retirement planning has changed fundamentally and permanently. A stool with shaky legs is no place you would want to sit. You need something sturdy and reliable. You need to develop a dependable income stream on your own. *It's up to you now.*

GOODBYE TO PENSIONS

Although many of today's retirees still receive pensions, the defined benefit plan is getting rarer among those now planning their retirement. Among retiring baby boomers, very few couples these days both have pensions; they have either one or none. If they do have a pension, they tend not to trust that it will be there to serve them throughout their retirement. They may lack confidence in whether the pension fund will remain solvent to fulfill its promise for a lifetime guarantee of a monthly check.

In fact, a lot of retirees opt to receive a lump sum in lieu of a monthly pension. It could make more sense to invest that money to produce an income. Typically, the income payout is higher with the pension, but you are giving up the asset to get that higher payout. Your pension might continue to cover your spouse after you die, but otherwise there are no beneficiary options at death. With your own investment or annuity, your heirs could get any remaining cash value. Like everything else, this decision needs to be made looking at all the options with a financial planner who specializes in retirement-income planning and in the context of an overall plan.

Increasingly, far fewer workers in the private sector are expecting any pension at all. Future retirees are not anticipating such a predictable source of income. A steadily dwindling percentage of them believe they can rely on the company, or on the government, to take care of them.

They are coming to terms with the fact that their personal investments and savings must fill the gap because they cannot depend on a pension or on Social Security. Today there is a lot more pressure on families to make sure that those savings are sufficient and that they will last a lifetime. It's the individual who now makes the investment decisions and takes on the risk. As 401(k)-type plans have replaced many companies' pensions in the last generation, the responsibility for retirement planning has shifted from the employer to the employee.

A SYSTEM IN TROUBLE

Social Security benefits are a major source of income for most retirees. The Social Security Administration's most recent statistics show that the benefits represent at least half of the retirement income for 48 percent of married couples and 71 percent of unmarried people. In the years ahead, however, the benefits likely will be making up an increasingly smaller portion of retirees' income needs.[2]

The Social Security system was never designed as the primary source of retirement income. When the system was established in the 1930s—in the midst of the Great Depression—it was intended as a safety net to help support the relatively few people who would not live for more than a short time into their retirement years. It was meant as a supplement to help keep the elderly population out of poverty.

The retirement age originally was set at sixty-five, but the life expectancy back then was only a few years longer. Today, the life expectancy for both men and women in the United States is approaching eighty years, and medical advances likely will continue to extend our life spans. The number of people who have celebrated their hundredth birthday has more than doubled in the last ten years. Today there are 125,000 centenarians in the United States. By the year 2050, it is projected that there will be over a million.[3] Retirees

2 "Social Security Administration Fact Sheet," Social Security Administration (December 2015), https://www.ssa.gov/news/press/factsheets/basicfact-alt.pdf.
3 "The SunAmerica Retirement Re-Set Study: Redefining retirement post recession," SunAmerica Financial Group, (July 2011), 12, https://fulltextreports.com/2011/07/14/the-sunamerica-retirement-re-set-study-redefining-retirement-post-recession/.

often draw benefits for three decades or more, nearly as long as they worked. That puts a tremendous strain on the system.

In addition, baby boomers today are entering their retirement years in droves. As a result, far fewer workers will be paying into the system to support many more retirees in the years ahead. The situation is already troubling. Consider these statistics, as reported by the Social Security Administration: In 1940, there were 159 workers for each beneficiary. That number has since fallen to fewer than three workers for each beneficiary, and the ratio is expected to fall to 2:1 over the next decade or two, according to projections.[4]

It's clear that the system is in trouble. The administration's latest estimate is that the Social Security trust fund will be depleted by 2035 to the point where the program will only have enough revenue coming in to pay seventy-seven cents for every dollar of retiree benefits that were promised. The revenue for disability payments is projected to dry up much sooner—and that's a part of the system that I believe often is abused, draining away funds that otherwise could have gone to retiree benefits. Unless something is done to shore up the system, it will self-destruct.

SOCIAL SECURITY'S FUTURE

How can Social Security be fixed? It's a highly politicized issue, and the changes that Congress makes likely will affect younger people much more than those who are approaching retirement or who have already crossed that threshold. I tell my clients that if they will be retiring in the next five to ten years, they probably can count on receiving much of what they were told they would get. I don't think

---

4 "Ratio of Covered Workers to Beneficiaries," Social Security Administration, https://www.ssa.gov/history/ratios.html.

that politicians will be taking money away from current retirees or from people who will soon be getting their benefit. They are likely to kick the issue down the road to make it a problem for a younger generation.

What we will probably be seeing are further increases in the full retirement age. For years, it was age sixty-five. It is currently age sixty-six for people born in 1954 or earlier. For people born after that, it increases in two-month increments until it reaches age sixty-seven for those born in 1960 or later. Some are proposing to increase the full retirement age to seventy.

I would not be surprised to see Social Security benefits subjected to "means testing," under which the benefit you receive would be based upon somebody else's notion of how badly you need the money. Such a "solution" would be a disincentive to save and would amount to punishing those who have done a good job of preparing for retirement. If you have made a lot of money in your career, you also have contributed more to the Social Security system. I feel you have a right to get that money back.

Other proposals could also be aimed at people earning higher incomes. Besides raising the actual Social Security tax itself, Congress could significantly increase, or even eliminate, the upper limit of income that can be taxed for Social Security, which is $127,200 for 2017.

Congress could also subject more of your Social Security benefit to income tax. Originally, the benefit was fully exempt, but now up to 85 percent can be taxed. That could rise even higher. First you pay a tax to be eligible for the benefit, and then you pay another tax when you get it. We could also see further changes such as the recent elimination of many of the file-and-suspend and similar strategies that couples have long used to enhance their spousal benefits.

Again, any major measures would not likely be aimed at those currently at or near retirement. Still, to be conservative in their financial planning, some people prefer to calculate a benefit that is less than the full amount that they are likely to get. After all, somewhere down the line, changes are coming. It's inevitable, considering the underlying issues and the demographics, so planning should be on the safe side.

You can be sure that those changes are not likely to mean more money in your pocket. The Social Security leg of the retirement stool will be getting ever weaker in the years ahead. The prevailing feeling among many people preparing for retirement is that they just can't count on Social Security any more than they could count on the pensions that once were the foundation of retirement planning.

WHEN TO TAKE SOCIAL SECURITY

One of the key factors in your retirement-income plan is determining the age at which you should begin taking your Social Security benefit. Should you take benefits at sixty-two or wait until your full retirement age? Or should you hold off on your benefits until you are seventy? Or would somewhere in between those years be best for you?

Your decision will have a significant impact on the amount of money that you will get for the rest of your life. Every year that you postpone your benefit, it will increase approximately 8 percent. A worker can choose to elect benefits as early as sixty-two, but doing so may result in a reduction of as much as 30 percent from your full retirement amount. If you wait until seventy, it can be as much as 32 percent more than at full-retirement age. Let's say you were born in 1954 and are eligible for $1,000 a month at your full retirement age of sixty-six. If you retire at sixty-two, your benefit would be $750. If you retire at age seventy, your benefit would be $1,320. It will not increase beyond that age.

Social Security		
Age	**Pros**	**Cons**
62	Receive benefits earlier	Smallest monthly check Possible reduction penalty if employed
Full Retirement Age	Higher monthly check No penalty if employed	No benefits age 62 to FRA
70	Highest monthly check No penalty if employed	No benefits age 62 to 70

Beware of basing your "Social Security timing decision" on some maximization report. As with any and all retirement planning decisions, make this decision in the context of your overall plan. For example, by waiting to take Social Security benefits, you will get more income later, but you may have to use up more of your own assets earlier. But also, if you take Social Security early, you will get less income later, but you may also use up less of your own assets earlier. Also, beware of basing your plan based on any Social Security "tricks" that may be available today but that may be gone tomorrow when you need it.

It's far from a simple decision. You need to carefully consider all the variables, not just the raw numbers. Also, your decision should take into account your health and life expectancy. And another key factor in the decision is whether or not you plan to continue to work after claiming retirement benefits from Social Security. If you elect benefits prior to your full retirement age and you continue to work, your benefits may be reduced. However, there is no reduction in benefits if you wait until at least full retirement age and continue to work and have earned income.

Do you intend to keep earning a significant income? Even if you aren't retiring early, you will need to carefully consider whether that income, when added to your Social Security benefit, pushes you into higher tax brackets. With much of the benefit already subject to taxation, you could lose even more of it.

How is your health? How long do your relatives tend to live? Those are important considerations because, to put it bluntly, you might want to grab the money while you can. If health concerns not only prevent you from working but also could cut your life short, you probably would rather have the money in hand sooner rather than later. Many people try to calculate the "break-even point" for their benefits. That's how long you would need to live before you would get the same amount of money whether you took Social Security retirement benefits early or waited. If you are in fragile health and your break-even point is years away, why wait?

If you are married, you also will want to consider the Social Security benefit for your spouse, if you pass away, also known as the survivor benefit. If both of you are getting a benefit, the survivor will continue with the higher of the two amounts. Let's say Bill gets $2,000 a month, and his wife, Jill, gets $1,000 a month, for a combined benefit of $3,000. If Bill dies, Jill in effect trades her benefit for Bill's—and the amount that Bill received was based on the age at which he chose to take benefits. If you take early retirement, you may be reducing your spouse's monthly income for many years after you are gone.

SOME IDEAS FOR SOCIAL SECURITY INCOME

I might recommend to a couple, for example, that the wife start her benefit at full-retirement age but that the husband wait until he is seventy to begin his. This strategy will leave the highest benefit for her in the future. They very well could gain an advantage this way instead of both of them taking their benefit at the same age. Whether that makes sense, though, will depend upon their age difference, how long each of them is likely to live, and other factors. For example, if they are particularly concerned that one of them might need custodial care, they might decide not to postpone their benefits so that they can use some of the money to pay the premiums on a long-term-care policy.

You may decide to draw your benefit early if you have plenty of other assets and would like to create a financial legacy for your family or for charity. Let's say you don't need your benefit. You have more than enough other income, and Social Security payments feel like a bonus to you. The right strategy could multiply your benefit many times. You could file to start receiving benefits, pay the tax, and then use the net proceeds to pay the premium on a life insurance policy, leaving the payout to the beneficiaries of your choice—such as your children. In that way, they are, in essence, inheriting your Social Security payments, and the money will be going to them tax-free.

As you can see, the decision is not as simple as answering a few generic questions in a retirement guidebook or punching figures into an online calculator to determine how to get the most from Social Security. You need to think long and hard before responding to that letter from the Social Security Administration that spells out your benefit options. No single answer fits everybody. The right choices lie in the balance of your needs, goals, personal circumstances, tax situation, health, marital status, your other assets and investment opportunities, your desire to leave a legacy, and whether you simply need the money to pay the bills. *The timing of your Social Security benefit needs to be part of a comprehensive plan.*

SHIFTING OF RESPONSIBILITY: THE 401(k) REVOLUTION

In 1978, Congress added an obscure provision to the tax code that was designed to offer a tax break on deferred income. A few years later, a benefits consultant named Ted Benna saw the possibilities: perhaps that provision could be extended to the workplace so that employees could save for retirement without being taxed, until they withdrew from their accounts years later. The IRS approved Benna's plan to create the first 401(k) plan with his employer, the Johnson Companies, where the workers began to contribute through salary deductions.

The concept was soon flourishing nationwide as many companies large and small created their own defined-contribution plans in the decades ahead. The plans offered an immediate income tax break to employees on the amount of their contributions, and the money could grow tax-deferred for decades. Some employers began offering a matching contribution to whatever the workers set aside. It was, in a sense, free money.

At the same time, those companies were shutting down their defined-benefit pension plans, and in so doing they were released from their expensive lifelong obligation to take care of former employees. The switch to 401(k)s also freed them from their responsibility to maintain the integrity of the pension fund. During economic downturns, when corporate earnings declined, the companies had to increase their contributions to those pension plans at the worst possible times for them. With 401(k)s, they could simply reduce or eliminate their profit-sharing contribution during tough years. As employers saw these significant advantages, the trend continued through the 1980s and 1990s.

Today, few companies continue to offer pensions, which now exist mostly in the public sector. The 401(k) and similar plans have become the primary means by which people save for retirement. Many have most of their money in these tax-deferred plans—and the company is no longer managing their investments for them. This has become the task of each employee. The responsibility to choose investments wisely now falls on him or her. The advantages are clear: the tax deduction and deferral can promote impressive growth, while the company match enhances those gains through the years. Also, these plans encourage people to develop the discipline of saving regularly and systematically, which is critical to building retirement security.

Unfortunately, many people do not have a clue how to invest appropriately. That is why the 401(k)-type plans are so highly regulated. Employers are considered to be fiduciaries who must offer a quality investment menu. Still, many people sock money away into these plans without any idea whether it's enough or whether they have made the right investment choices. They just contribute a random amount into an investment they don't really understand and hope for the best. The company encourages their participation in the plan, but too often it doesn't equip them to choose wisely.

If they were to go to a qualified financial planner, they could find out relatively easily whether they were saving sufficiently—depending on what they envision their life will be like in retirement. Once they know that, figuring out the allocations needed to get there is the easy part. There's no need to invest blindly, although that is what many people do. Some just choose the same funds that a coworker recommends—although that coworker may be in an entirely different stage of life with different priorities, needs, and goals.

Instead, you should align yourself with someone who can lead you the right way. Employees are in great need of financial education. To advance that, I go into workplaces to do workshops and help employees find the answers to their questions. The 401(k)-investment custodian, who just helps them choose an asset allocation, is not the right source for these answers. Plan participants need objective advice from a professional who focuses on retirement-income planning. Employers who provide financial education to their employees do them a good service and show that they really care.

Employers often feel that their 401(k) provider already offers such advice, but the provider's job is just to get as many people to participate as possible. That's good, of course, but the provider is not looking at the endgame for each individual investor. A qualified financial planner will get to know the retirement goals and income needs of a client—and employers would do well to make that kind of objective, independent financial advice available to their employees.

But it's ultimately up to *you*—not only to make sure you have accumulated enough but also to make sure you preserve it and plan so that you can provide a lifetime income. Knowledge is critical to success. In this new era when the government and your employer are less likely to take care of you in retirement, you must make your own investment decisions. The wrong advice could doom your retirement hopes. The right advice can lead you to your dreams.

CHAPTER 3

The Planning Process

Start with the end in mind. This is common advice—and yet it is central and essential to retirement success. You will hear it repeated in one way or another throughout this book. As you approach retirement, the years of just putting money aside to watch it grow are ending. We must make the most of our lives. We should set our sights on a vision and then daily seek the wisdom to advance there. It is high time to find the point of it all.

I had a client once tell me that she wanted me to put together a plan that would allow her to retire "tomorrow." In other words, she wanted to know that if she decided to stop working at any time from that day forward, she would be able to do so without fear. She did not have a plan, even though she had saved very well over the course of her professional career. After careful planning, I put together a retirement-income plan that gave her tremendous peace of mind, and she was confident that she could retire at any time in the future and have the income and lifestyle she desired—all from having a plan. In fact, it worked so well that even as of this writing—several years later—she is still hard at work! It was just the confidence of *knowing*. That's what a plan can do.

I have also seen the consequences of failing to set life goals. Some couples indulge themselves as they pursue dreams that their portfolios could never support. Other couples with impressive portfolios are unduly frugal out of fear that they could lose it all—and end up losing out on memories. Either way, they are in need of wisdom. Good financial habits should be developed long before retirement. People who spend impulsively throughout their lives are unlikely to change much when they retire. Fearful people often stay fearful. The lack of discipline and perspective leads to trouble.

I have worked with couples who seem determined to spend more than they make. Even after we design a financial plan, they make monthly requests for big withdrawals that tap into money that they had designated for longer-term needs, such as a hedge against inflation or taxes or health-care expenses. Or they try to raid their liquid emergency fund when there is no emergency. They are just overspending and indulging. For now, they have a reliable income, but they are robbing their future. They need to learn to number their days.

My responsibility is to help keep my clients stay on track, and that starts with the proper planning up front. With a plan in place, I can remind them of the purpose that they themselves defined for their money. They can do as they wish with their dollars, of course, but my job is to explain what will happen if they continue along a path that strays away from the plan.

I also sometimes remind nervous clients that they can go out and enjoy life because their portfolio and their plan are in great shape. "Yes, you can take that trip," I reassure them. "It's certainly not going to get in the way of reaching your goals." The unknown can be frightening. It is sad to see people counting pennies or worrying about the stock market every day when they have reached a point in life of true financial freedom. By having a plan, they gain reassurance. They can see how their investments support their vision; *clarity and simplicity can be the cure for underspending as well as overspending.*

WHAT DOES RETIREMENT LOOK LIKE TO YOU?

What is it all about? That is a question increasingly on the minds of people as they get older. Why did they work so hard all those years— to what end? As they rushed about trying to get their promotions and raise their families, they may not have paused to think much about it. By the time they reach retirement age, though, they need to clarify their life goals. They need a context for their finances.

This is a fundamental discussion that comes early in my relationship with clients and that precedes any specific investment recommendations or strategies. How they define their life goals will determine the nature of their planning. It will govern their decisions on estate planning and tax management. It will influence how they deal with the many financial risks they will face. If I made investment recommendations with a client in our first meeting, I would not be putting "wisdom first."

It reminds me of the following dialogue from *Alice in Wonderland:*

Cat: Where are you going?

Alice: Which way should I go?

Cat: That depends on where you are going.

Alice: I don't know.

Cat: Then it doesn't matter which way you go.

It matters "which way you go." What does retirement look like to you? That's where we must start if we are to develop a financial plan that encompasses all your needs and wants. A solid and reliable financial plan starts with the big picture. What is your vision for this stage of life? How will you know when you have reached your goal? Unless you know where you are going, you will wander aimlessly along the byways of life or you will be constantly changing directions.

Retirement is about living a full life, not just managing a portfolio. It is important to identify and pursue a purpose in retirement—and that purpose can be grand or modest. We inhabit a wide world of many needs, and retirees are well suited to fill them. With their wisdom and experience, retirees have much to offer to society for years to come.

As Mitch Anthony emphasizes in his book *The New Retirementality*, we need not say farewell to our creative lives. Retirees are in a great position to pursue a cause and make a difference. Many people have started new careers or launched new businesses or remained involved to their profession as consultants and mentors. Some will serve by sitting on boards and committees, and others will serve by babysitting the grandchildren. Both are important contributions, and both (some would say the latter in particular) keep the mind and body active.

A TRUE FINANCIAL PLAN

What constitutes a financial plan? I have found that many people are confused about that. They tell me that they have a plan because they own an annuity or have a portfolio of mutual funds or a 401(k). They tell me that their plan is to successfully invest so that their portfolio reaches $1 million, or $10 million, or whatever number they have determined will provide them with security. That is their hope—but hope is not a plan, nor is any particular financial product; nor does a plan arise from the answers to some questionnaire.

A true plan is a guide to your dreams. It is custom-fitted and as unique as you and your family. It is based on your values, vision, and goals for retirement and the legacy that you desire to leave to the next generations. The plan plots out the course for your goals. It involves your money, certainly, but a lot more. A plan is about life and living it well.

We start, then, by getting a grip on your priorities in life. A pile of money without purpose is just paper. What matters is how you can use it to attain what you want to accomplish. Ask yourself, who is important to you and what causes matter most? Where have you dreamed of traveling? Do you have any desires to reinvent yourself in a new career, perhaps? Do you want to learn new things? Do you want to contribute to your grandchildren's education? How much importance do you place in your ability to leave money to charity, or to your loved ones? There is no point in counting your dollars unless you consider what they can do for you and for others.

A plan is not a plan until it is written down. It can't be something that you have only thought about. A written plan brings clarity and at the same time can easily be shared with others as needed. That said, I have seen financial plans that are hundreds of pages in length and covered in leather binders, but that is not necessary. A simple plan that is easy to read and understand is what works best. I try to create financial plans on one sheet of paper, if at all possible. It does not need to be complex; there is great value in simplicity (thus the name of this book!). The plan should be simple, while the strategies and investment options may be more involved.

NO MAGIC NUMBER

Your dreams and visions for retirement need to be in line with your resources, and so your financial plan needs to make sure you can achieve them. Once you have identified your retirement and life objectives, it is time to get real. The time will come during your financial planning when you must make sure that the money is there to meet your expectations.

A lot of people would like me to be able to just pull out a calculator and tally their various savings and investment accounts and tell them whether they have reached some magic number that will give them peace of mind. It is never that easy.

Everybody's number is different, and it must be based upon what retirement looks like to the individual or couple. Do you prefer to stay close to home, for example, or are you world travelers? Do you intend to spend down much of their assets during retirement, or do you want to leave a hefty sum to their children and/or to charities? In other words, we are back to that fundamental question: *What does retirement look like to you?*

Once you can answer that question, then you can quantify it. A couple might tell me, "We have lived in this house for thirty years, and this is where we feel happy. We don't need to travel much—but we do want to fix up the place and put in a pool so that we can enjoy it even more when the kids and grandkids come to visit." Their retirement goals are rather clear, and we can set about figuring those costs and the timeline. Another couple might tell me they want to sell their house, buy a motorhome, and travel the country, visiting their children and grandchildren in various locales from coast to coast. Other retirees want to golf daily or explore the world.

Whatever the pursuit, once we know it, we can put a number to it. The second key question, therefore, after determining what retirement looks like to you, is this: *How much is that going to cost?* When you can answer that question, you will bring your financial planning into much better focus.

It starts with a simple budget. We need not get too detailed at first: I provide a one-page sheet that clients can use as a template for estimating the major spending categories of retirement—food, shelter, clothing, transportation, travel, utilities, insurances, gifts

Estimate Your Monthly Retirement Expenses

Living Expenses	Monthly Cost	Lifestyle Expenses	Monthly Cost
Housing *e.g. mortgage payments, real insurance, property tax*		Entertainment *e.g. movies, theater, sporting events and restaurants*	
Utilities *e.g. gas, water, electricity, telephone, cable*		Travel & Recreation *e.g. hotels, airfare and RV/boat expenses*	
Food/Groceries/Meals		Memberships *e.g. golf, health club and yoga*	
Transportation *e.g. car payments, gas, car insurance, maintenance*		Gifts and Donations	
Personal *e.g. clothing, haircuts, dry cleaning, toiletries*		Other	
Health Care *e.g. medical insurance, vision/dental, prescriptions and other out-of-pocket expenses*		Monthly Lifestyle Expenses	
Life, Disability, and Long-Term Care Insurance		Monthly Living Expenses	
Other		Monthly Lifestyle Expenses	
Monthly Living Expenses		Total Expenses *(Monthly Living + Lifestyle)*	

Guaranteed Retirement Income Savings

Owner	Source *(Social Security/ Pension/Annuity)*	Monthly Amount
	Total	

and more. From there we can see the approximate size of any financial gap that needs to be filled. We can become much more specific about those living expenses, if necessary, and then we can calculate the lifestyle expenses.

Retirees tend to spend more in the early years of retirement than later, and that's just a matter of energy. They have things to cross off the "bucket list," a term popularized by a movie of that name, starring Jack Nicholson and Morgan Freeman as two terminally ill men who take a road trip of adventure. Many people postpone trips and activities throughout their working years, and then, during the first decade or so of retirement, they try to make up for lost time. Later, health considerations may get in the way, but more often than not, they just get to the point where they feel that three trips to Hawaii, for instance, are probably enough!

The nature of the risks that retirees face also evolves. Early in retirement, the biggest risk for many is spending too much. Spending tends to become less of an issue later, but other issues—inflation, taxes, health-care expenses—rise to the forefront. The level of spending actually can increase later in retirement for those reasons. It is variable, based upon needs and conditions. Retiree spending generally will be greater at first, level for a while, and then rise again.

DETERMINE *YOUR* INCOME NUMBER

A commonly prescribed rule of thumb is that your retirement income should be 80 percent of what it was before you left your job. It is an arbitrary number that ignores individuality. It also ignores the fact that retirees have widely differing expectations. In reality, many people will need just as much income, if not more. They may have moved beyond some expenses—perhaps they have paid off the mortgage, for example—but other expenses have come along to take their place. A great many retirees travel extensively, particularly in the first several years. Golf fees add up quickly! Before retirement, much of the discretionary spending took place on weekends. Now, every day is like a weekend!

Later in retirement, you are sure to feel the effects of inflation, unless your financial plan compensates for it. Taxes, too, must play a role in the planning because they are likely to rise from historical lows. Health-care costs will mount, not only due to inflation but also due to the inevitable infirmities of age. How then can anyone expect that the 80 percent rule will hold true? It is yet another dubious guideline that tries to offer a magic number. You must arrive at *your number* through careful consideration. Your income number is the basis for your whole plan, so make sure you think through *all* your retirement expenses. This is not easy to do and therefore causes many people to do nothing. So my advice is to determine an income-number goal and then adjust it as needed. But there can be no plan or recommendations until a retirement-income number is first established.

You need to identify two levels of income: your *living* expenses and your *lifestyle* expenses. You will have certain expenses that will not be discretionary or that you will consider not to be. You will need a roof over your head, you will need to eat, and you will need transportation, for example. You must pay utility bills, taxes, and certain insurances. Those are the expenses that you will be paying every month, no matter what. Your list might include costs that others would consider optional, but to you they are necessities of life—tithing, for example. These are your *living expenses.*

Life is more than paying the bills, however. You are certain to find other ways to spend your money. You will want to do things like dine out, buy gifts, go on a special vacation, join the golf club, donate to charity. These are your *lifestyle expenses*. Again, there is overlap between the living and the lifestyle expenses, depending on what you personally deem to be essential. Once you have identified and differentiated them, though, you can calculate a number for both.

TAKE TIME TO PRACTICE

Once you have arrived at a number that makes sense for your retirement-income requirements, I highly recommend that you practice living on that number. During the six months before you retire, limit all your spending to only that amount. Before committing yourself, see whether your number truly works for you.

By practicing to live on that amount prior to retirement, you can determine whether your resources are up to the task of paying for all that you would like to do during retirement. You will soon see whether you have enough to support both categories or whether you might need to guarantee an income that will cover only your living expenses. That does not mean the rest is beyond your reach, but you may want to base those expenses upon how well the market performs for you in a particular year. Maybe you can put off that dream trip for a year or two. Or maybe you will find that you have more than enough to ensure that you can meet your needs (living expenses) and your wants (lifestyle expenses) for the rest of your days.

GETTING ORGANIZED

As I begin meeting with prospective clients, they often bring along a load of documents. Those are certainly important, but as you can see they will not be the initial focus of conversation. We cannot dive into the financial statements until we discover the life priorities. This is what we call the soft data, which involves those questions about the vision for retirement and how much they wish to leave behind. Some want to maximize the use of their money during their lifetime, and others want to leave as much as possible to their heirs.

After that brainstorming, we can get to the hard data. This is the gathering stage where we look closely at available resources. We examine the types of accounts and investments currently owned and whether they are serving their best purpose. We examine 401(k), IRA, and brokerage statements and determine how and by whom they are owned. Is there a joint ownership? Is the money in a trust? We look at the account values in banks. We find out about any annuities, life insurance, and other insurance policies. In addition, I want to see how any trusts are titled, and we will want to review whether the beneficiaries have been updated.

Once we gather and analyze all this information, we can determine whether the assets are sufficient to accomplish the stated goals. We may suggest that certain accounts be consolidated for the sake of simplicity. At that time, we would also be able to make specific recommendations about which accounts should be used to cover your income needs.

We provide a summary document that shows the specifics of every account. We recommend that all this information be kept in a safe or other secure location and that they make sure their loved ones know where to find it, if necessary. In addition to that, we provide an online "vault" on our investment platform for secure document storage. Our clients can put a digital copy of any of their documents in that vault, or we can do that for them.

A PLACE FOR BOTH SPOUSES

I do my utmost to make sure that if my clients are married that both spouses are involved in the planning process. If a prospective client were to tell me, "My wife doesn't care about this stuff, so it's just going to be me," I would still require that she come to some of the meetings. I will not do a retirement-income plan based on information and feedback provided from just one spouse.

Each has a crucial perspective. For example, the husband might be the one who is primarily interested in the finances, but the wife is more in touch with the family relationships—and those, as we have seen, play no small role in the nature of the planning. He may prefer to use up all the family assets during their lifetime, but she may emphasize the importance of leaving some assets for the children and grandkids. She may well have a different view on how they should proceed, and they need to come together for a unified plan.

Unless husband and wife stand united, the plan can easily fall apart. One of the spouses might indeed truly be the silent partner who trusts the other with all decisions and does not care to hear the recommendations. However, he or she still needs to fully understand the game plan and agree with the purposes for the allocations.

Also, I want to make sure that both spouses know how to access information on all their accounts, since most of the time the surviving spouse is the one left to deal with those financial details. The children are preoccupied with their own family pressures, careers, and other priorities. Therefore, at least both spouses need to be aware of the financial-planning details, although it is always a good idea if at least one other person is apprised.

PROCRASTINATORS, BEWARE!

Perhaps the biggest risk to launching a successful retirement plan is the human propensity for procrastination. The first step can be the hardest. The task can seem overwhelming to contemplate, and families may fear that uncomfortable issues will arise. As a result, they may fail to deal with important matters, such as outdated beneficiaries on a 401(k) plan or insurance policy. Ex-spouses have been known to stake a claim because the documents were never reviewed and updated.

When people are afraid of what they will see, they try not to look. If you are overweight, you may not want to look in the mirror—but how does that help your situation? If you do not shine a light into the darkness, you might not see an obstacle, but it is far more likely to trip you up.

Many people harbor a deep fear that they have not saved enough and that they have blown their chances for a comfortable retirement. Fear is a powerful emotion. It leads people astray in the marketplace, and it can paralyze them so that they do not even get started in planning the course of their lives. And it leads some to believe that they cannot trust anyone for clear, honest advice. They do not know where to find someone who will be on their side and show them the way. Instead, they try to do it on their own, and the mistakes pile up.

My advice is this: Once you take a look, then you will know what changes you need to make. Awareness leads to action. One of the key lessons I've learned in business is that *success comes from activity, not from analysis.* You can always formulate some sort of action plan. For example, the plan might be that you need to work an additional four years or that you need to reduce your spending. Perhaps you may decide that an increased level of market risk would be acceptable so that you might gain a higher rate of return.

You can be sure that there will be something that you can do, once you face up to the fact that you have an issue. Ignoring it will worsen it. Ask yourself this: If something were threatening the future happiness of you and your family, how soon would you want to know about it? Right away, most likely. If your goal is to retire at age sixty-five, then you need to know at age fifty-five whether you are on track. You don't want to wait until you are sixty-three and then regret what you failed to do several years earlier.

Retirement planning, in other words, should start as soon as possible. There is no such thing as starting too soon. The sooner you can get on track, and stay there, the better off you will be. Good planning calls for vigilance. It is what you do not know that can hurt you most. You cannot overcome if you do not see what is coming.

I had a client who found out less than two years after we had done all the retirement and financial planning for him and his wife that he had developed a serious medical condition that would have rendered him uninsurable. But since he and his wife did not procrastinate and had acted years earlier, he had already acquired ample amounts of insurance not only to provide tax-free income in the future but also to protect against future long-term care expense risk and to leave a sizable amount to his heirs. His current health condition has no effect on his prior planning.

An experienced financial planner who focuses on retirement-income planning can help to make sure that you are not caught by surprise. With a plan in place, you can start with the end in mind and work backward, choosing the investments and products that fit your purposes. The plan will give you a firm grasp of your resources and what you can realistically do with them. The key is in the organization—you must organize your priorities, and you must get your documents and paperwork in order—and you must do so without delay.

AN INVESTMENT IN WISDOM

I think of the words of Jeremiah the prophet: "What will you do in the end thereof?" We are called upon to consider what "the end" looks like and to make sure that we get the right things into place. Ben Franklin said it well, "An investment in knowledge pays the best interest." Life is short, so the time to plan is now. You cannot put it off. You cannot wait to secure a legacy for your family. By making an investment in wisdom, you can achieve true wealth a.k.a. financial peace for you and your family.

CHAPTER 4

Risks That Require Attention

"I pulled all my money out of the market before the crash," I have heard people say with a look of self-satisfaction, as if their wise timing spared them the financial turmoil that countless investors experienced in the severe recession that began in 2008.

"That's great!" I say. "And when did you get back in?" Sometimes they never really did, and they missed out on a remarkable recovery, which, as I write this, has endured more than seven years, one of the longest on record. Though the pace of growth has been slow, those who endured the crash but stayed in the game likely made more overall than those who bailed out for good.

Such is the nature of market risk. You can lose if you do and lose if you don't. The nature of your risk has much to do with your investment phase of life: An economic downturn just before or during retirement, when you are preserving and distributing your money, can hurt you far more than during your working years of accumulation. That is why I put so much emphasis earlier in this book on understanding those phases. If you are at the point where retirement is in sight, or you already have launched into it, market volatility will have a major impact not only on your portfolio but also on your peace of mind.

Risk management, however, involves more than the markets and investments. Most people think that managing risk is all about finding just the right asset allocation. It is that but also so much more. Retirees must deal with inflation, fluctuating interest rates, taxes, hidden fees, and medical and long-term-care costs. No matter what financial products you own, you cannot be ready for retirement unless you have addressed those risks.

You face financial threats on multiple fronts, all of which could diminish your future income. One of my five principles that I shared in the introduction to this book is: *protect the income; grow the rest.* In other words, if you are going to take a risk, it should be with money that you can afford to lose. In chapter 7, we will discuss income planning in detail, but it is important to understand from the start that income planning and risk management go hand in hand.

Too much is at stake to leave it to chance, particularly in retirement, when you and your portfolio are particularly vulnerable. In this chapter, we will take a closer look at some of those threats to peace of mind. Later chapters will examine two major ones: taxation and the potentially devastating cost of long-term care.

AVERAGE VS. REAL RATE OF RETURN

Let's say you had invested $1 million in the market. The first year you lose 10 percent, and the second year you gain 10 percent—and that pattern repeats itself for a decade, with 10 percent losses and 10 percent gains in alternate years. How much would you have in the end?

You might believe that you would break even. After all, the average rate of return for those ten years comes out to zero, so clearly you gained nothing. But that does not mean that you lost nothing. You would end the decade with $950,990.05. You would have taken a loss of $49,009.95, or 4.9 percent.

Average vs. Actual Rate of Return

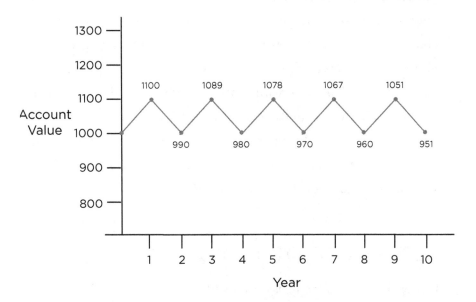

The math is clear. The average rate of return over a period of time does not equate to your real, personal rate of return for that same period, if there are any negative returns thrown into the mix.

Another example: You invest $100,000 in a mutual fund for two years, and the first year it loses 50 percent and in the second year it gains 50 percent. Your average annual rate of return is zero, but you would have suffered a loss of $25,000. Your investment is down by 25 percent.

Think about this long and hard—*the average annual rate of return never equals the real rate of return over time if there are ever any negative returns mixed in.* This is an extremely important concept to come to terms with because it directly affects what investments you should use to draw income from in retirement.

People tend to be impressed if they learn that some mutual fund has averaged a 6 percent annual rate of return over the last forty years. If you plan to withdraw 4 percent a year, that sounds like a good place to put your money. But it doesn't work that way. It would only work if you were getting a fixed rate of return of 6 percent every year, guaranteed. However, that 6 percent is an average, which means some years the fund might have been down 10 percent and other years up 15 percent, with a variety of other annual performance results. Logically, it sounds good—average 6 percent and withdraw 4 percent and you will never run out of money. But it is simply not always true—it does not always work out that way. This is because of something called "sequence-of-returns" risk.

SEQUENCE OF RETURNS

If your retirement income is dependent upon an account that fluctuates with the market, it is essential that the sequence of returns fall in your favor. If the economy delivers a blow to your investments early in retirement while you are starting to withdraw money from that account, you might never recover. Your savings could evaporate.

See the following chart for an example of how this works. There are two couples—Dave and Joan and also Jeff and Wendy. They both start off retirement with a balance of $500,000, they each *average* a 6 percent annual return on their investments over their lifetime, and they each *withdraw* 5 percent of their balance annually adjusted for inflation. As you will notice, Dave and Joan ran out of money in thirteen years! But Jeff and Wendy not only did not run out of money

DAVE AND JOAN				JEFF AND WENDY		
Sequence of returns: Poor, then strong				Sequence of returns: Strong, then poor		
Hypothetical New Return	Withdrawal	Balance	AGE	Hypothetical New Return	Withdrawal	Balance
		$500,000	65			$500,000
-27.1%	$25,000	346,275	66	26.7%	$25,000	601,825
-16.5%	25,750	267,638	67	10.1%	25,750	634,259
-1.9%	26,523	236,535	68	4.3%	26,523	633,869
3.1%	27,318	215,702	69	8.9%	27,318	660,534
10.9%	28,138	208,009	70	17.6%	28,138	743,697
-9.4%	28,982	162,199	71	22.5%	28,982	875,527
7.4%	29,851	142,141	72	-3.7%	29,851	814,385
8.1%	30,747	120,417	73	18.1%	30,747	925,477
15.4%	31,669	102,415	74	-6.1%	31,669	839,286
9.4%	32,619	76,356	75	9.2%	32,619	880,880
6.2%	33,598	45,410	76	7.6%	33,598	911,675
12.4%	34,606	12,143	77	9.6%	34,606	961,268
2.8%	12,143	0	78	22.4%	35,644	1,132,964
11.4%	0	0	79	-11.0%	36,713	975,663
9.0%	0	0	80	24.3%	37,815	1,165,745
24.3%	0	0	81	9.0%	38,949	1,288,207
-11.0%	0	0	82	11.4%	40,118	1,323,532
22.4%	0	0	83	2.8%	41,321	1,318,113
9.6%	0	0	84	12.4%	42,561	1,433,720
7.6%	0	0	85	6.2%	43,838	1,476,055
9.2%	0	0	86	9.4%	45,153	1,565,407
-6.1%	0	0	87	15.4%	46,507	1,752,811
18.1%	0	0	88	8.1%	47,903	1,843,006
-3.7%	0	0	89	7.4%	49,340	1,926,397
22.5%	0	0	90	-9.4%	50,820	1,699,273
17.6%	0	0	91	10.9%	52,344	1,826,444
8.9%	0	0	92	3.1%	53,915	1,827,478
4.3%	0	0	93	-1.9%	55,532	1,738,278
10.1%	0	0	94	-16.5%	57,198	1,403,702
26.7%	0	0	95	-27.1%	58,914	980,350
	Average Annual Net Return 6%				Average Annual Net Return 6%	

but their accounts grew. How is this possible? It is the *sequence of the returns.* Dave and Joan had poor investment returns early but better later when it was too late. But Jeff and Wendy had better returns early and poor later when it didn't really matter. Which one will represent you? No one knows, but it is an extremely important risk to address in a retirement-income plan.

The point here is that you can't just blindly choose a portfolio with a long history of average annual rates of return of 6 percent or more and then just assume that as long as your annual withdrawal rate is below that, then you will automatically be okay. This is one of the biggest mistakes that retirees make.

If you talk to Dave and Joan, they would tell you not to leave all your money exposed to market risk in retirement, because you will run out of money. And they would be right. If you talk to Jeff and Wendy, they would say that you should leave all your money exposed to market risk in retirement because you will never run out of money and actually still gain . . . and they would be right too. Both couples would be telling the truth based on their own personal experiences. Both of these scenarios are possible. This is why it is also extremely important *not* to base your own retirement-investment decisions on the experience of someone else or do it the way someone else did it just because it worked for them. It may have worked or not worked for them, but that does not mean that it will work or not work for you.

The point here is that you must realize that you can't just accept stated "average annual rates of returns" and that you must also decide how you are going to manage against a very real, yet most often overlooked retirement-income risk—"sequence of returns." I will discuss in a later chapter how we recommend our clients mitigate against this risk. It's one of our core principles—*protect the income; grow the rest.*

This is another paradigm shift that prospective retirees must acknowledge. You are moving from the days when you were building your retirement portfolio to the days when you will be using it. Earlier in life, the sequence of returns did not matter as much. Now it plays a critical role. It presents a real risk that must be addressed. If you are depending upon stock-market performance for retirement income, you may be gambling with your future.

The sequence of returns only matters if you are withdrawing money or taking income. The order of the returns didn't matter very much during the accumulation phase (most of your investing life), but now suddenly it does. Still, many financial advisors will make a simple statement such as this: "Mr. and Mrs. Jones, if you average 6 percent per year in this portfolio and you withdraw 5 percent every year, you should not run out of money in retirement." It sounds as if it must be true. Logically, it makes sense. But as you can see, it is an illusion. If the average rate of return includes any losing years, it will not be the same as the real rate of return that you actually experience. That's the case even if you never withdraw a cent.

Later in the book we will explore the "three-bucket approach" to retirement-income planning that I recommend to my clients. Sequence-of-returns risk needs to be addressed in the "income-bucket" portion of the retirement-income portfolio because it is uniquely associated with distribution, but it will not be as much of a concern in the "growth-bucket" portion, since no regular withdrawals will be planned from there.

DIVERSIFICATION

To invest wisely, you need to properly diversify your assets. It's the wisdom of Solomon: "Divide your portion to seven, or even to eight," we read in Ecclesiastes 11:2, "for you do not know what misfortune may occur on the earth." How do you know if your portfolio is diversified? Most people mistake being diversified for owning a bunch of different stuff. But you could have investments in several mutual funds with a lot of overlap in those investments. Perhaps they're all US large-cap funds. They're all doing pretty much the same thing. Your only diversification there is within that one asset class.

For a portfolio to be truly diversified, the asset classes within it should have low correlation with one another. In other words, they should react differently, with almost an inverse effect. Think of sunscreen and an umbrella. Typically, there is an inverse relationship between the two—if I need sunscreen, I don't need an umbrella and when I need an umbrella, I don't need sunscreen. This is how asset classes in a portfolio should react to one another. When one is lagging, another is surging ahead. Historically, certain asset classes have had low correlation with others, although at times they all seem correlated—as in 2008, when they all joined in the slide. So the way to lower the risk, or standard deviation, of a portfolio is to reduce the correlation among the assets within it.

Your asset allocation will be based on the rate of return that you need in order to meet the objectives that you have identified. *Your aim will be to take the least amount of risk possible to obtain that return*, choosing the appropriate asset classes. Over time, however, some of those asset classes will perform better than others. Unless you act, they will soon represent a disproportionately large share of your portfolio.

Rebalancing is the process of getting the asset mix back in line with your original intentions and your risk tolerance. It helps to keep you in the discipline of selling high and buying low. Let's say that you decided on a mix of 60 percent stocks and 40 percent bonds. You also wanted a certain percentage of your stocks in international equities, a certain percentage in emerging markets, and the remainder in US companies. You notice after a few years that the US equities make up a larger piece of the pie, by virtue of their consistent performance. As tough as it might seem to do, it's time to sell off some of the gains from your winners and use the proceeds to buy more stock in your weaker performers at a bargain price. How often should you do that? Some suggest quarterly, but I believe it's wise to let the winners have more of a run and rebalance annually.

You should only put at risk, however, what you can afford to lose—and once you have determined that amount, you should remain committed to that decision. You either believe in the market in the long term, or you do not. If you are investing money for growth to meet future needs and to deal with inflation and tax increases, then you should not be constantly getting in and getting out on the market. After all, in any given year, most of the returns can be attributed to just a few days—and missing even one or two of them will have a dramatic impact on your return. Nobody knows in advance which days those will be. Market timing simply does not work. Long-term commitment does.

FIVE-YEAR RULE

Even though moving money around in the short term feels good, it doesn't produce better results long term. When investing in the market, you should always take a long-term view. An independent research firm called DALBAR, Inc. has done many studies that compare the average rates of return of major stock-market index benchmarks (S&P 500, etc.) with the returns of the average investor, and in every case the indexes beat the return of the average investor.

How is that possible? It's because average investors tend to chase returns or act emotionally with their investments, causing them to make short-term decisions based on fear and greed. There is a real cost associated with that approach—not just in long-term returns.

A better approach is to look at any investment in the stock market as a long-term investment. So, for me, long term is five years or longer. I always remind my clients of my "five-year rule": *If you need the money or access to the money within five years, we should not take a risk with it, but if you have no plans to access the funds within five years, then we should take some market risk with it.* Of course, when I say put it at risk, I mean taking the least amount of risk for the rate of return you need, which is done through proper asset allocation and diversification as we touched on earlier.

The point is that by only putting money at risk that you don't need for five years or longer allows you not to have to react to short-term market conditions. I don't necessarily concern myself with how a portfolio performs over a week, a month, or even a couple of years—I am most concerned with the performance of a given portfolio over five years and longer. This approach allows you to stay diversified and disciplined. If you add in rebalancing, this is a prudent long-term approach, which has been historically proven to outperform. It's not always easy to do, but that's why choosing a financial advisor who also has a long-term view and coaches you on the perils of emotional investing or having a short-term outlook is extremely valuable in the long run.

Stock-market investing is ideal in the "accumulation phase" of investing because time is on your side. It also works well in the "growth-bucket" portion of the retirement-income portfolio (three-bucket approach) that we will talk about later in this book. The reason is the same for both—the time frame for needing access to those funds is five years or longer.

INFLATION RISK

During your working years, inflation may not be much of a worry. You more than likely get regular pay raises that tend to keep pace with it. When you are on a fixed income in retirement, however, the impact of inflation matters much more to you. Unless you can create your own raises, it will erode your purchasing power. For seniors, inflation can be even worse than for the general consumer. The Bureau of Labor Statistics created a separate index that tracks the health-care and shelter expenses that disproportionately erode the buying power of older citizens.

Inflation, as I have pointed out, is one of the *big three* among the risks that you will face in retirement, along with health-care costs and taxes. To keep on top of it, you need sufficient growth in your retirement portfolio to overcome its effects. You shouldn't be ultraconservative with all your retirement assets out of fear of losing them. You will still be losing if your portfolio's rate of growth falls short of the inflation rate. You can beat it only if you put some portion of your money at risk. It needs to be a diversified risk, however, that you take only with an amount that you can afford to expose that way—and your return, of course, needs to outpace inflation.

Once upon a time in the late 1970s and early '80s, certificates of deposit commanded impressive interest rates. Those were the days of double-digit inflation rates as well, during the Gerald Ford and Jimmy Carter administrations. CDs have never been an effective hedge against inflation, but that is not their purpose. They are not designed to beat inflation. Their proper function in a portfolio is to keep your money safe—so CDs may be a good place for emergency funds and money that you will need in the short term. For example, if you are planning to buy a car in a year or two, CDs will give you a modest return in the meantime without risking your principal.

If you are planning to wait to buy your next car in five or ten years, however, you need a much better rate of return. The cost of a new car today is probably about the same as what you paid for your first house, if you are of retirement age. Since 1900, inflation has averaged about 3 percent.

Think about what you paid for a loaf of bread, or a postage stamp, or a movie ticket in 1989. What will you be paying when that much time has passed again? You can be sure those price increases aren't going to stop. Inflation isn't going away. Even at a modest inflation rate of 2.5 percent, the cost of goods will double over twenty-eight years. Back when time spent in retirement was relatively brief, inflation wasn't as much of a concern. Today's retirees need investments that are up to the task of seeing them through many more years. Over the course of one's years in retirement, they could very easily see things cost twice as much at the end of their life as they did at the beginning of their retirement! This is something that must be addressed in your retirement-income plan. I address it in the "growth-bucket" portion of our three-bucket approach.

INTEREST-RATE RISK

When some CD rates were nearly 18 percent for a time in mid-1981, you could invest $1 million and expect $180,000 in annual income, secure from market risk. If you were retiring then, you might have felt that CDs were all the investment you would ever need, despite the rampant inflation. But those rates were soon to plunge. A year later, CD rates were under 10 percent. A decade later, they were about 5 percent. Recently they have been about 1 percent, or a $10,000 payout on that same million dollars. Meanwhile, inflation and taxation keep gnawing away.

If you had depended upon CDs all those years for your retirement income, you would have had to steadily decrease your standard of living. Imagine that you had a job in 1981 paying $180,000 and the boss slashed your salary every year until you were earning just $10,000. That is one way to illustrate the concept of interest-rate risk. You cannot be certain of the direction that interest rates will take in the years ahead. If you are pinning your retirement to a rate expectation, you could be in for quite a downfall.

The risk of fluctuating interest rates is a major concern for bond investors. The big risk right now is in the potential that rates will increase, thereby diminishing the value of their existing holdings. Bond values and interest rates have an inverse relationship. As one rises, the other falls, as if they were on opposite ends of a seesaw. Rising rates naturally will erode the value of existing bonds because investors will seek better yields elsewhere. Falling interest rates, by contrast, will make those fixed rates on the older bonds more attractive.

Interest rates have recently been at historic lows. They will be rising, most economists believe, and they will be correct about that eventually—because, after all, where else can the rates go? They disagree on how soon. If you are buying bonds in such an environment, you should be very careful about the duration. Long-term bonds make more sense to buy when rates are high and are expected to drop and you want to lock in a good rate. With better rates on the horizon, though, long-term bonds could lock you into a low return and keep you from pursuing investments with a higher return.

Shorter-term bonds at least would let you buy into those rates as they rise. Bond investors in an environment like this often "ladder" their purchases so that money becomes available every year to take advantage of rising rates.

INVESTMENT-FEE RISK

Many people are only vaguely aware, if at all, of the internal expenses that drain away a significant portion of the return on their mutual funds. This is a huge issue, since those funds represent a major portion of the retirement dollars invested in 401(k) plans. The participants in those plans, however, are sometimes under the impression that they are not paying any fees on the money in their 401(k) plans.

Every fund comes with some sort of cost. Those managers and administrators and custodians and record keepers and others are not doing it for free. You can see the posted expense ratio for every fund in its prospectus, but some costs are harder to see. There are fees paid to broker-dealers for agreeing to use the funds—in other words, kickbacks to the brokerage firms. There are also the trading costs for the buying and selling that goes on within the fund. If the fund has 100 percent turnover, that means every investment within it changed during the year. Each of those trades incurs a cost.

How can you learn more about those fund fees? Almost every fund has what is called a statement of additional information. Most people are aware only of the expense ratios in the prospectus. This additional document, however, breaks down all the fees within a fund. It is available by request from your financial institution, or your advisor can get it for you. It helps to clarify how much you are paying to participate in the fund and how much the expenses detract from the return.

A fiduciary advisor can help you get a true picture of all those expenses. If you're working with a fee-based advisor, he or she will have a vested interest in the value of your portfolio. When I look at my clients' portfolios, I am just as concerned as they might be about the expense ratio of the funds. I care about the turnover and custodial costs. That is because our interests are aligned. We both benefit by maximizing the return.

Although we strive to keep those expenses as low as possible, that does not mean that the fund with the lowest fees is necessarily the best. Let's say a fund has an expense that is twenty basis points higher than another, but its returns are regularly 1 percent greater. Both are US large-cap funds, so you would think they are doing the same thing and, therefore, the one with lower expense ratios would perform better. But that is not always the case. Generally, you want the lowest costs overall to maximize your returns—but the fund with the lowest fees may not always be your best performer.

LONGEVITY RISK

To live a long, prosperous life would seem to be the ideal. You worked hard for decades to position your family for a comfortable retirement. You want to make the most of what could be the best years of your life. And yet surveys have indicated that the greatest fear among many people of retirement age is that they will outlive their assets. What's wrong here?

It's not that older people have lost the will to live. On the contrary, countless retirees show the world daily how much they can offer. The word "retirement," in fact, is somewhat misleading, since many remain highly active and engaged. What they are lacking, all too often, is *financial* confidence. They fear that they will run out of money before they run out of years.

If we lived only a short time beyond our working years, the risks that we have examined in this chapter would not matter so much. Our longevity accentuates the potential impact of those risks. Why do we care about inflation? Because we are living long enough to feel how it can drag us down. Why do we care how the stock and bond markets perform? Because our investments need to serve us well for many years to come. As we will see in the chapters ahead, we must also manage taxation effectively and confront the risk of long-term care so that they do not deplete our savings that must last a lifetime.

With diligent planning that addresses all these risks, you need not worry about outliving your assets. Using my three-bucket approach (see chapter 7) and following the principles outlined in this book, you can enjoy a long and fulfilling retirement with peace of mind.

CHAPTER 5

Taxes on Your Terms

Taxation hits us from all directions, it seems—on our income and purchases, on our property and capital gains, and more. It might feel as if the only escape from taxes is death, but don't forget the estate tax. The government may want a piece of you then, too, particularly if you have built up substantial wealth.

From a historic perspective, though, we are nowhere near the all-time high for income taxes. In the war years of 1944–45, the upper brackets were 90 percent on incomes between a hundred thousand and two hundred thousand and 94 percent on incomes over that. The lowest bracket was 23 percent on incomes under $2,000. Throughout the 1950s and early '60s, the top bracket stayed above 90 percent. It was 70 percent throughout the 1970s. Compare those tax rates with today's top bracket of 39.6 percent.

If you consider our national debt and deficit spending and the troubled state of the Social Security system, you may reasonably conclude that tax rates are highly likely to revert to something closer to the historic average. The typical means by which people are saving for retirement these days is through tax-deferred plans such as 401(k)s and traditional IRAs. As baby boomers reach the age when they must

U.S. income tax rates for highest-income earners

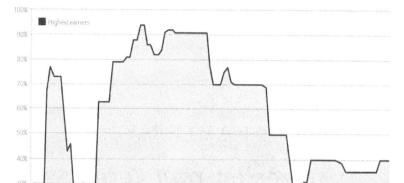

withdraw those savings, the government will be eager to finally claim its cut of that huge pool of resources.

Taxation clearly remains one of the biggest risks that people face in retirement. A comprehensive financial plan must anticipate the consequences of future rate increases.

TAX STATUS OF ASSETS

The assets in a portfolio will be made up of some combination of three basic categories: taxable, tax-deferred, and tax-free. Ideally, that mix should be determined by an overall strategy and purpose for those investments. Let's take a closer look at each.

Summary	Fully-Taxable	Tax-Deferred	Tax-Free
Current investment balance	$100,000	$100,000	$100,000
Annual contributions	$0	$0	$0
Number of years to invest	20	20	20
Before-tax return	6.5%	6.5%	6.5%
Marginal tax bracket	28%	28%	28%
After-tax return	4.7%	6.5%	6.5%
Future account value	$249,617	$352,365	$352,365
Future account value (after tax)	$249,617	$281,702	$352,365

TAX-DEFERRED INVESTMENTS

Investments in this category—primarily, the trillions of dollars in 401(k)s and traditional IRAs are not subject to taxation until those dollars are withdrawn in retirement. You pay no tax on the growth of the account all those years, and you also get a tax deduction each year that equals the amount of your contributions. That frees up your resources so that you can potentially save even more.

These accounts can help you avoid a lot of upfront taxes during your working career, and they can grow to substantial size by the time you are ready to retire. That's a mixed blessing, however, because simultaneously you have acquired a major tax liability. Once you turn 70½ years old, it's time to start paying up. You can no longer sit on all that money. You will have required minimum distributions every year, and those long-postponed taxes will then be due at the prevailing income tax rate. The presumption is that the tax rate, and your tax bracket, will be lower when you retire. Those presumptions may be wrong.

Tax-deferred investments limit your liquidity. If you withdraw any money before age 59½, not only must you pay the taxes due on it but you also will incur a 10 percent penalty except under very limited conditions. If for some reason, you fail to make those required annual withdrawals after age 70½, your penalty on top of your taxes will be a staggering 50 percent of the amount you were supposed to take out.

TAX-FREE INVESTMENTS

It's easy to see the big advantage of an investment in which you never pay a tax on the growth, but this is also the category where people tend to have the least amount of retirement savings. The options for true tax-free investing are limited, and you get no income tax deduction on the front end.

The most commonly cited assets for producing tax-free income include specially designed life insurance policies, investments held in Roth IRAs, and municipal bonds. Of those, municipal bonds are often not 100 percent income tax-free; they may be free of federal but not state tax, or vice versa. Municipal bond interest payments count as provisional income when calculating Social Security tax and may be subject to capital gains tax when sold.

Specially designed life insurance policies are ideal for people who have at least ten years to fund the policy or to defer before drawing income. There are no income restrictions, and contribution limits can be much higher than with Roth IRAs. Future income is taken out as a loan from the insurer while your cash value continues to grow throughout your lifetime.

The tax-free Roth has the advantage of greater liquidity. You can withdraw your *contributions*—although not your earnings—at any time. You do not have to wait until you are age 59½ to do so. However, in order to withdraw your *earnings* tax-free, you will need to wait at least five years and be at least age 59½. The Roth also comes with a substantial long-term tax advantage because you don't have the mandatory age 70½ required minimum distributions of the traditional IRA and 401(k)-type plans.

TAXABLE INVESTMENTS

These are investments that are taxed annually on whatever they earn. You will get a Form 1099 notice each year for taxes due on dividends, interest, or capital gains. They can include stocks and bonds, mutual funds, CDs, and your bank accounts. They have the advantage of liquidity over tax-deferred accounts, which often cannot be accessed until age 59½.

You will not get a tax deduction on the money you put in these investments, but you do gain flexibility. You have a pool of investment money that you can tap for whatever you wish, without penalty, even if you are years away from the typical retirement age. Perhaps you intend to retire early. Maybe you are saving for a major purchase or want to help your children and grandchildren with college or other expenses.

WHERE TO SAVE FOR RETIREMENT?

People often ask me about the types of accounts and investments they should be using for their retirement savings. What is the best combination of taxable, tax-deferred, and tax-free investing? Generally, it is important to have all three types of investments so that you have more flexibility to maximize your income and minimize your tax obligations during retirement. The right combination, of course, depends upon the individual, but I can offer some guidelines.

Generally, I suggest that *you first should accept any "free" money that your employer is offering.* By that, I mean don't pass up any matching amount that you could get to your contributions to a 401(k)-type plan. The employer match amounts to a 100 percent return on your investment. Even though the money will be fully taxable one of these days, you still can't beat that.

Once you have contributed up to the maximum match, then you should consider tax-free investments. Primarily, that will be money that you can put into a **Roth IRA**. In recent years, some employers have been offering tax-free Roth accounts as part of their 401(k) plans. These are good retirement-investment options, up to the point where you reach your contribution limit. Again, you will not get an annual tax deduction for your contributions, but the ability to grow the account without ever incurring income tax is a huge advantage.

You may also wish to invest in **life insurance**, which potentially can produce tax-free income when structured the right way. Basically, you are overfunding the policy. If you qualify, the IRS allows you to invest more than the premium cost of the death benefit. The investments inside the policy grow tax-deferred, and eventually you can withdraw the money as loans from the insurance company, which amounts to a tax-free income. Eventually the cash value of the policy should grow sufficiently to repay the loans and still offer a death benefit for the family. It's a strategy that makes sense, so long as you have at least a decade to pursue it. Generally, you can invest more into a life insurance policy without the contribution limits of the Roth IRA.

After you have made the most of those strategies, I suggest returning to your tax-deferred accounts for further investments beyond the company match. Although you will be creating a tax liability for the future, you will still be getting your annual deductions, your investments will grow tax-deferred, and you will be saving in a systematic and disciplined manner that is essential to building wealth. At that point, *if you still want to save even more for retirement and add flexibility and liquidity to your plan, you could also consider taxable accounts.*

WHERE TO DRAW INCOME FROM?

Another common question involves the order in which you should withdraw money from those various accounts during retirement to get the greatest tax advantage. In other words, how can you produce the most income with the least amount of tax? If you are getting Social Security and pension money as well, what is the best strategy?

The right tax strategy will depend on many factors, including your age, how much money you need, how much money you have and where it is invested, and how those investments are performing. A key consideration for many will be the required distribution that will become a progressively larger portion of their income. Those RMDs should be managed in the context of a comprehensive financial plan. There is no simple answer, but if you do this right, you can save significantly on taxes.

When I have clients who will not be needing those RMDs or using the money for regular income, I may suggest that they use whatever proceeds remain after paying the tax on each withdrawal to purchase life insurance. "I don't need this IRA," they may tell me, "so I'm just going to leave it to the kids." A better idea may be to use a life insurance policy to multiply those dollars. That way, the kids will be inheriting the tax-free death benefit. Basically, this strategy is a way of cashing in the IRA over time so that the kids can inherit the life insurance policy instead of the IRA.

CONVERTING TO A ROTH

Many people who have invested for years in a traditional IRA or a 401(k) look with envy at the advantages of the tax-free Roth and wonder how they might take advantage of it. They consider the possibility of "buying out" the government—that is converting their tax-deferred savings into a tax-free account like a Roth IRA or a life insurance policy.

You can convert, but first you must give the government its due. For example, you can transfer funds from a traditional IRA directly into a Roth IRA, but you will owe the deferred tax that you should pay out of pocket on each amount that you convert and each year that you convert. Even though you will incur taxes by converting an IRA directly into a Roth IRA, you will not have to pay a penalty even if you convert prior to age 59½. *You cannot escape the taxes, but you can escape the penalty and the uncertainty of what the future might hold.* You know what you owe today and what you can afford to pay in taxes now. Who knows what taxes will be tomorrow as your account continues to grow and the government continues to spend.

That tax obligation that you have pushed down the road so long can be intimidating, but many people who convert to a Roth do so a little at a time, year by year, starting well before retirement. To do the conversion, you must start with a traditional IRA, but if you have a 401(k) it is easy to roll the funds directly into one. It generally is far better to convert gradually so that you can keep your tax bracket as low as possible each year. To convert to a Roth all at once would likely put you in the highest bracket unless your account is relatively small.

A gradual conversion also allows you to pay the tax at your own pace under your own terms instead of waiting to let the government decide how much it will take and when. I have often worked with clients to do such conversions. It is a means of eliminating risk. Once you have converted to a Roth, those RMDs are no longer an issue, and you no longer are at the mercy of how much politicians may decide to raise taxes.

Converting is not for everyone, however. Let's say you are sixty-five, ready to retire, and all your money is in 401(k)s and IRAs. After preparing an income plan, we find out that it will take most of your money in those accounts to generate what you need to live on. You would not have enough additional assets to use for income while doing a conversion over five to ten years. In that case, the conversion would not make sense.

Generally, however, *you should strive to convert tax-deferred accounts into tax-free accounts—as much as you can, as often as you can, and as soon as you can.* For the most part, you cannot move money out of your existing 401(k) at your current employer until you are at least 59½, but you *can* convert your traditional IRAs and old 401(k) from former employers.

401(k) PROS AND CONS

I'm not trying to suggest that you should steer clear of 401(k)-type plans and traditional IRAs. As I pointed out earlier, the company match in a 401(k) is free money. It doesn't get any better than that. And these plans are an easy way to save, through payroll deductions. Some companies will automatically enroll you. You set money aside regularly and systematically, before you even see it, and you do get that annual tax deduction for the contributions. Were it not for the 401(k), many people in this post-pension era would have nothing to show for retirement.

Another big advantage of the 401(k) is that the contribution limits are relatively high, and generally, there are no income limits as there are with the traditional and the Roth IRAs. If you are under age fifty, your 401(k) contribution limit is currently $18,000 a year, and it is $24,000 a year if you are over fifty. The maximums for a traditional IRA or a Roth are $5,500 for under age fifty and $6,500 for over age fifty. If you are in a position where you need to be saving more for retirement, your only choice might be your 401(k) because of those higher contribution limits.

Also, many companies now offer Roth-401(k)s, which allow you to make your contributions into a Roth account. You will not get to deduct your contributions, but your account will grow tax-deferred and may be withdrawn in the future tax-free.

The downside of 401(k) plans is that the investment decisions are on you, the risk is all yours, and you determine the outcome—but you cannot do anything about the taxes and how much the government eventually might decide to take. That is why it might be better to pay out of pocket for a conversion to a Roth if and when possible rather than to leave future taxes to chance. That's a risk that must not be ignored.

That is why you may also want to find out if your company allows what is called an age 59½ "in-service distribution." This is a non-hardship withdrawal that many 401(k) plans allow so that employees can look outside of their current plan offerings for other investments that may better meet the needs of the employee. This is an opportunity that most, if not all, of my clients have taken advantage of. Even though you are still employed and are still contributing to the plan, with no plans of retiring any time soon, this provision just allows you to take some or all of whatever you have saved so far and roll it over to an IRA so that you can have control of the investments. It's very important that you do this as a direct rollover—meaning the funds move directly from the 401(k) and into an IRA so that you avoid any income tax obligations. Get advice and help from a qualified financial advisor before you do this.

When it comes to tax management, my job is to help my clients save for the long term. I look beyond this year's tax savings to see where they will stand years into the future. I recommend paying a known amount of tax on the seed rather than an unknown amount of tax on the harvest.

CUTTING THROUGH THE CONFUSION

Our nation's tax provisions can boggle even the experts. The federal tax laws and regulations have grown to more than ten million words, filling thousands upon thousands of pages. Among those provisions of the Internal Revenue Code are a variety of tax breaks. They are there for good reason, generally. Often, they are aimed at stimulating investment and promoting such things as home ownership and charitable giving that our society sees fit to encourage.

To determine how best to tame your taxes, you need the help of a professional who is well versed on strategies that work and has seen what fails. An IRS agent certainly is not going to show up at your door to tell you that you are paying more in taxes than necessary. You need to either find out for yourself how you can do better or work with somebody who is working in your best interest—not just for today but for tomorrow.

CHAPTER 6

Long-Term Caring

When I was in my twenties, a few years after I moved out of the house where I grew up, my grandfather moved in. He no longer could look after himself, and my mother and aunts were determined to take care of him for as long as he lived. They felt it was a matter of duty.

Our house was in Rhode Island and my aunts were in Kansas City, but they decided that they would take turns. Their plan was that my grandfather would live for a time at each of his daughters' homes.

Not only were the logistics difficult but it was no easy job. He had to be helped in and out of bed, and he was much bigger than my mom. It took an emotional toll as well: it was painful to witness the decline, day by day, of the man whom the family long had known as the strong provider.

Once, what my family did for my grandfather was common practice. When you got old and frail of body or mind, your spouse served as your caretaker for as long as possible, and then you moved in with the children. That was the expectation, almost an obligation.

When the kids were growing up, you took care of them, and now the time had come for them to take care of you. And they, too, considered that to be the right thing to do.

In today's society, two things have changed. The aging baby boomers often are reluctant to have their children become their caretakers. They are embarrassed at the prospect of being so dependent. The other major issue is that far more often, the children can't readily serve as the caretakers. Both spouses are working and raising families, with hectic lives already, and often they have put down roots hundreds of miles away. As much as they want to help, it can be a strategic struggle—as my mother and her sisters discovered.

Those societal shifts have resulted in today's common attitude that caring parents don't expect the kids to be their caretakers. They recognize the mental, physical, and emotional weight of that responsibility. They look for alternatives: home care, assisted-living communities, and the traditional nursing homes.

All of those come at quite a cost. Health-care expenses in general are particularly hard on seniors, who are often trying to get by on some combination of fixed income from Social Security, a pension, or an annuity. As those costs continue to outpace the overall inflation rate, retirees find that these costs take up an ever-increasing portion of the family budget. Medicare premiums have been rising faster than the Social Security cost-of-living adjustments, and Medicare doesn't cover everything. Out-of-pocket medical expenses alone can feel overwhelming over the course of retirement. And if either or both spouses need long-term care, the expense can have a dramatic impact on their life savings.

The good news is that a comprehensive financial plan will anticipate long-term-care risk and find effective means of dealing with it. There is no doubt that this is a huge threat to financial security.

Illness can devastate portfolios as well as dreams. Like the other big financial threats in retirement, we must carefully manage against long-term-care risk. And, like the others, unless you have addressed it you cannot truly say that you have a financial plan at all.

By addressing these risks well in advance, you are sparing your loved ones a lot of expense—and heartache. If you have seen friends and relatives struggle with the long-term-care issue, you will be less likely to postpone dealing with it. You will want to face it head on. If you think it won't happen in your family, consider this: According to the Genworth 2015 Cost of Care Survey, at least 70 percent of people who have reached age sixty-five will need long-term-care services of some sort during their lifetime.[5] You must not ignore this potential risk, no matter how healthy and strong you feel today. There are basically four ways to handle this risk: family and friends taking care of you, the government taking care of you (Medicaid), you taking care of your own expenses (self-insure), or transferring the risk to an insurance company (buy insurance).

IS MEDICARE OR MEDICAID AN OPTION?

It is a mistake to think Medicare will cover long-term-care costs. Medicare may pay for the first ninety days if you are transferred from a hospital to a rehab facility, but if you stay in the facility longer than that, those expenses may no longer be covered by Medicare. Generally, if you cannot perform two of the six activities of daily

---

5   "Genworth 2015 Cost of Care Survey," Genworth Financial, Inc., https://www.genworth.com/dam/Americas/US/PDFs/Consumer/corporate/130568_040115_gnw.pdf.

living, or if you have dementia, the staff will qualify you as a long-term-care case—and Medicare won't pay.

Like Social Security, Medicare is a program in financial distress. In fact, under current conditions, the Medicare fund is expected to dry up even sooner than the Social Security fund. It is not likely that benefits are going to get more generous. Medicare wants to stop paying pretty much as soon as it can. This means that long-term-care expenses are your own responsibility. You must make those payments out of pocket. Long-term care in an assisted-living facility costs about $4,500 a month, on average, and it can be much higher in other regions. Of course, the price also reflects the level and quality of care.

The burden of those payments, depending on how long they continue, can exhaust a retirement portfolio. That is when the state Medicaid system will kick in. The conditions are strict. Generally, you can only have a few thousand dollars of assets left, and you may be able to keep your house and car if your spouse is still living at home. If the household income is too high, you won't qualify. Each state differs on the details.

If Medicaid is paying the bills, the system is also going to decide the quality and location of your care; you lose that choice. You may be less than pleased with the decisions of a welfare program that by its nature strives to control costs. In a lot of ways, long-term-care risk is not only a financial risk but also a quality-of-care risk.

Some people take steps in advance so that they can present themselves on paper as penniless. In that way, they can qualify themselves for Medicaid from the day that they need the care. That calls for careful timing: The government will look back five years at the flow of your finances. If you have transferred money away within five years—to your children, perhaps, or into an irrevocable trust that you cannot control—you will not qualify for Medicaid until you have spent that amount on your long-term care. In effect, you must pay it back.

Any earlier transfers generally won't be considered, but most people don't act until they face the need—and it is hard to foresee that need so far in advance. Nor do they relish the thought of losing control of their life savings. And this is far from an easy strategy. The government may discover that your children are paying you $2,000 a month even though they got your assets seven years ago. "It is still your money," you may be told. The government expects that the assets you gave away, even earlier than five years, are no longer benefiting you—and that may be a hard picture to paint.

SELF-INSURANCE

Another way to handle long-term-care risks is to earmark some of your retirement assets toward paying for it. This may be the most expensive way to do it in the long run, but it is still a potential way to deal with this risk.

If a typical skilled nursing facility costs $5,000 per month and the average length of a long-term-care stay is three years, then it could potentially cost $180,000 (not counting inflation) to cover the cost for just one person. If you want to self-insure for two people, you may need to set aside $360,000.

There is not necessarily a problem with doing this, except for the fact that you render these funds illiquid and unavailable for any other use during your lifetime, so that it is always available in case of a future long-term-care need. The advantage of this approach, however, is that there is no medical underwriting involved and there are no premium payments to make. And if you never need long-term care, your heirs can inherit these funds through your estate.

Since people who consider this approach have enough money to pay out of pocket, they instead ought to consider purchasing a single-premium life-insurance policy that offers a return of premium if the buyer decides to end the coverage sometime later. This can be a much more efficient means of self-funding. You are leveraging the power of insurance and maximizing the use of your cash while keeping control.

Here is an example of how this works. Let's say you tell me that you are considering self-funding. You have enough money to set aside $360,000 to pay for long-term-care expenses, if they arise. You decide to earmark that money for long-term care and invest it for growth to offset inflation. I explain that, instead, you could purchase a single-premium policy, pay $150,000 up front, and get one and a half times that amount as a death benefit and two and a half times that amount as a long-term-care benefit. In other words, you would get $375,000 if you needed long-term care; otherwise, your heirs would receive $225,000 as a death benefit (tax-free by the way). If you decide to drop the coverage in the future, you could get your $150,000 premium back. The return-of-premium feature addresses a common complaint against traditional long-term-care insurance. People often object to paying a premium and losing that money forever when they might never need that kind of care.

Such a policy may serve you well. When you compare it with self-funding, you can cover your risk for a lot less money. And all the while, you maintain control of the asset. If you can afford it, I recommend this approach because you are, in essence, just repositioning assets. When I describe these policies, most people tell me they had no idea they were an option. Many of them see it as a huge opportunity. It's important to note, however, that since this is a life insurance policy, some medical underwriting will be involved.

INSURANCE ALTERNATIVES

Other than spending down your life savings so that you might qualify for Medicaid, or setting aside a large chunk of retirement assets to self-insure or to purchase a single-premium policy as described earlier, you could buy insurance where you pay monthly or annual premiums.

When you buy insurance, you are paying to transfer risk. By comparison, you are paying a little to insure against a much larger potential expense. It's interesting to me that the only time I ever hear clients talk about "wasted premiums" is usually in relation to a discussion about long-term-care insurance. We buy homeowners insurance and auto insurance too, but I don't hear people talking about paying for something and never getting anything in return, in that context. You certainly don't expect your house to burn or your car to crash, but since you know such things can happen and are out of your control, you pay to protect against the potential for major loss—and hope you never actually have to "cash in." You should think of long-term-care insurance in the same way.

TRADITIONAL LONG-TERM-CARE INSURANCE

If you qualify, you pay a monthly or annual premium for insurance that covers you only if you have a long-term-care need—including, in most recent policies, professional health care in your home. Typically, you will choose a monthly amount of coverage and a specific amount of time (e.g., $5,000 per month for three years), which would produce a maximum benefit in my example of $180,000. Based on your age, health, and those aforementioned variables, a premium amount will be set. You generally pay premiums for the insurance up and until you start claims against it and then the premium payments end.

My major concern with traditional long-term-care insurance is that the insurance companies do not quote a fixed rate. The premiums can, and do, go up over time. In your attempt to deal with a risk, you are taking on the new risk of an unknown future cost that is outside of your control. Several of my clients recently got letters telling them that their traditional long-term-care insurance premiums would be rising by 50 percent. It became a much greater expense than they had budgeted. Some people who have been paying for years feel forced to drop their coverage or to accept less coverage for the same premium.

LIFE INSURANCE WITH A LONG-TERM-CARE RIDER

To avoid that prospect, you may be able to obtain a hybrid life-insurance policy that will pay for long-term care if necessary. I like this option for two reasons. First, if you never need long-term care, your heirs receive a tax-free death benefit. One way or the other, your premiums will produce a payout, and you avoid the so-called "wasted-premium" concern. Secondly, because this is generally a guaranteed universal life-insurance policy, the premium is fixed for life and should never go up. You can budget with confidence. Not only that, but as inflation keeps boosting the cost of care, that fixed premium represents a greater value.

However, as with traditional long-term-care insurance, the hybrid life insurance policies require medical underwriting. If your health is such that you would not qualify, you might consider an annuity with a long-term-care rider. Let's say you are getting lifetime income of $20,000 a year from an annuity-income rider with a long-term-care feature. The rider might double that amount to $40,000 a year while you are in a long-term-care facility. That double payment would continue until you use up the cash value in the annuity contract, at which point it would revert to the guaranteed-lifetime-income amount. The advantage here is that there would be no health underwriting, but the insurers would still look at your finances to make sure the policy is suitable.

COMBINATION STRATEGIES

These various approaches are often used in various combinations to cover long-term-care risk. How they are combined depends upon your situation as well as your family history. For example, a couple might want more coverage for the wife if both of her parents had Alzheimer's. If there is a considerable age difference between spouses, the younger might decide to take care of the other, if that time comes.

A couple also might decide to cover only half the long-term-care risk. They may choose to buy less insurance, figuring they could pay out-of-pocket for the remaining cost using other assets. If necessary, they eventually could go on Medicaid, but planning ahead would make that less likely. It is a calculated risk—but when such a variety of alternatives are available, I see no sense in purposefully spending down all your money just so you can go on Medicaid. Even if you were to put $200,000 of your savings into an annuity with a 5 percent lifetime income payout, you would have $10,000 a year for life to use toward the premiums for traditional long-term-care insurance. To earmark that $200,000 would seem a better strategy than spending down all your assets.

You could also take advantage of your state's partnership plan, which is designed to encourage you to buy long-term-care insurance. If you have a qualified policy that eventually pays out for long-term care, every dollar of that benefit that is paid out is a dollar more of your assets that you will be allowed to preserve and still get Medicaid coverage. So if the insurance company pays a family $200,000 in long-term-care benefits, the family will be allowed to retain an additional $200,000 in assets while still qualifying for Medicaid. The state recognizes that your purchase of long-term-care insurance saved taxpayers a lot of money. When most people buy a policy, they obtain coverage for three years—and since the average stay in a facility is 2.8 years, Medicaid never kicks in.

CARING FOR THE LONG TERM

However you choose to deal with the risk of long-term care, be sure that you don't just brush it off. Remember, one of my key principles is: *Don't let your portfolio take a HIT.* The "H" is for health-care expenses, and the biggest of those could well be the custodial care that so many families need. You must not ignore a risk that represents one of the main reasons that people run out of money in retirement.

Procrastination on this issue is understandable—but unacceptable. Nobody wants to imagine themselves or loved ones in a state of decline, but to ignore this risk not only could compromise your life savings but your family relationships as well. If you act now, you can protect the money that you have been hoping will one day go to your children. If you take no action, your children may have to stand by helplessly as that money drains away.

How will they feel when they know that you could have prevented that? By procrastinating, you risk planting the seeds of guilt and resentment. The children may feel bad enough that they can't take care of you at home—and now, each time they come to visit you, it occurs to them that their inheritance is evaporating.

That's not ingratitude; it's just human nature, and many families have experienced such tensions. You *can* do something about it.

As you weigh the options that we have examined in this chapter, you may decide to deal with long-term-care risk through your growth portfolio, saving money and setting it aside in case it is needed for that purpose; or you may decide to deal with it through your income strategy, making sure you have enough money coming in to pay an insurance premium. Your family circumstances will determine the right direction, but in one way or another you must confront this huge risk.

Think of it this way: when you face up to the fact that one day you might need long-term care, you are expressing how much you care about your family for the long term. Or another way to put it: don't forget about the *care* in long-term-care planning.

CHAPTER 7

A Three-Bucket Approach

T here was a time in my life when I would have been thrilled if someone had called me to say, "Hey, I have $100,000 to invest, and I trust you to do whatever you want to do with it." I know that I quickly could have found some solution, depending on my employment at the time. In fact, my allegiance as a salesman was to my employer, not to the investor.

The best advice I can give you at this point is that you should work with an advisor who cares enough to find out what your goals are and for what purpose you want to invest your funds and for how long. Today, I never give any recommendations during the first meeting with a new client. That is the time to be gathering information, looking at the possibilities, thinking it through, and beginning to consider the options that make sense. The recommendations come later. The wisdom must come first.

The very name of my firm, Wise Wealth, reflects my philosophy that wisdom must precede wealth. I believe that people should not base their trust in me simply on the fact that I am a fiduciary and they like what they have heard. That isn't enough; they need to know that I understand their situation enough to help them in the best way possible. Yes, I am required by law and by ethics to act in their best interests—but I can't presume to do that unless I find out just what those interests are.

Here's a simple rule: you should *never make investment decisions outside the context of a plan*—and you should feel reassured when an advisor refuses to make any recommendations outside that context.

There are things to consider before making investment recommendations and decisions. To help you do this right, I start with a lot of questions so that I can understand your goals. For what purpose is the money? Do you need the money to be liquid and accessible, or is your priority to see it grow, or is it to produce income? To what extent are you trying to preserve this money? Where are your other assets, and how are they invested? How much of it is liquid, and how much of it is currently invested at risk?

I am sure you will recognize those themes as ones that we have been touching upon throughout this book. In this chapter, we will take a closer look at how it all comes together. We will look at the logistics of planning your retirement finances so that you will have a reliable lifetime income, as well as sufficient money for short-term expenses, emergencies, and long-term expenses. I will explain the three "buckets" of retirement planning—your liquid, income, and growth buckets.

I recently spoke with a woman who was looking to roll over about $300,000 that she had invested in a 403(b) account. She had sizable assets beyond that amount, but she was clear that she did not want me to take that into consideration. "This 403(b) account is the only thing that I want you to worry about," she told me. "That's the only place where I want to hear your opinion and ideas, so let's just keep it to that."

"If we just keep it to that, though," I told her, "I would be concerned that I might misguide you. I might suggest that you do something that you are already doing elsewhere, or I might put you in investments that duplicate what you already have so that you have too much in one place and aren't diversified." I told her that if we were to work together, at the very least I would need to see her other financial statements at our next meeting.

In effect, she was asking me to make recommendations out of context. That is not what I do. I put things *into* context—of your other finances and your life goals.

For a long time, I have noticed that people often have investment products in their portfolio mix that seem to have no rhyme or reason. When I ask my prospective clients why they own these things, I hear things like, "it sounded good at the time," or "my brother recommended it," or my favorite—"I have no idea!" There is no justification for why they have this product or that one.

When salespeople try to sell you something based on limited information, you are likely to feel that they are taking advantage of you—and yet they can be so persuasive that you end up with a portfolio of products that suit the purposes of someone other than yourself. You could end up with five accounts with the same types of investments. Nobody has analyzed those accounts to look for overlap or lack of true diversification. Nobody has designated those investments for a specific use. Nobody has put a purpose to your portfolio.

PROTECT THE INCOME; GROW THE REST

In this book's introduction, we looked at the concept of *"protect the income; grow the rest,"* which I consider to be a governing principle of sound financial planning. A central aim of comprehensive planning should be to develop a retirement income that will be secure for a lifetime.

I had a client who sold a business and had plenty of assets to enjoy a comfortable retirement. However, since he had never really put together a plan there was still a nagging sense that he might not "make it." Once we put together a plan that protected his income stream, he and his wife had peace of mind. And now, after several years, they still have never withdrawn a dime. It was the peace of mind of knowing that they were protected that they needed more than anything else.

Most people would agree that they should protect the amount of assets from their portfolio needed to produce an income stream while seeking to grow the rest of it—but then they try to do all of that within a single portfolio or using one investment. Truthfully, that is impossible. No single investment or portfolio can accomplish the broad purposes of keeping money liquid, keeping it safe, growing it, and drawing an income stream from it.

What I recommend instead is allocation based on *purpose*. If your purpose is to have accessible money for near-term purchases and expenses, then let's find the products designed for liquidity. If your purpose is to produce income, then let's find the investments designed for income. If your purpose is for long-term growth, let's find the investments that are designed for growth. This is an approach that works. *Allocating assets based on purpose is more efficient, less expensive, and brings you peace of mind.*

Different people have different priorities. Some want to protect only the amount of money they need for their living expenses while allowing their "wants," or lifestyle expenses, to be at risk in the market. Others want 100 percent protection for both their living and lifestyle expenses. And still others are willing to risk it all so that they might seek greater growth.

Retirement Portfolio

Liquid	Income	Growth
Emergency fund *Known purchases/expenses within the next 3-5 years *Liquid	*Assets required to produce desired retirement income for life *Not-liquid	*For future income needs as well as future purchases *Help offset inflation, taxes, and healthcare expenses *Liquid

Those who do the latter, however, are either ignoring or are unaware of the foundational principle that you should first set aside enough resources to protect your income and then grow the rest. The income that you will need in retirement should not be at the mercy of the market. Instead, you should aim to find the least amount of risk needed to generate enough money to meet your standard of living. That is why it is so important to identify those expenses and do the overall planning before diving into the investment choices.

How much income do you need? That is the first question to answer, and many people have only a vague idea about that. As a result, they live in fear of running out of money—or they spend without recognizing that danger is imminent. I feel that a major part of my job is to help people stay true to their plan, whether I need to tell them, "You can't keep spending like this," or, "You are doing just fine, feel free to take that vacation." Someone who knows you well and understands your plan will be able to hold you accountable to managing your money prudently.

Once you have identified your retirement-income need, then you can determine the amount of assets that will be required to generate it. You should protect whatever amount that turns out to be. What you do with the remainder of your money is up to your discretion. You can take on riskier investments or not, but in any case you will not be affecting your income stream. That portion is already out of the equation.

As a full-service provider, my firm can objectively make recommendations on what is right for your needs and for the right reasons. You need to allocate your resources so that you account for each of the unique risks that you will face in retirement (see chapter 4). You want to choose the best products to meet your needs and manage your risks.

That is the essence of my three-bucket approach to retirement planning. All three buckets have their place, providing either liquidity, income, or growth, but none of them is all-purpose. The trick to successfully planning for retirement is to keep them in their right place and to use them as they are meant to be used.

Let's take a closer look at the significance of each of those buckets and the rules that should govern them. Keep in mind this principle about the nature of investments in general: they are designed to offer either safety, liquidity, or growth. Most investments will provide any two of those, in varying degrees, but relatively little of the third. That is a fundamental about the nature of investments that will determine what will fit best within each of your buckets. Before getting into the details of each bucket, please take a moment and watch a short video that explains how the three buckets work. You can view the video at www.wisewealth.com/three-buckets/.

THE LIQUID BUCKET

Liquid

This bucket contains readily accessible money for two purposes, primarily. You want enough money for an emergency fund that represents at least three to six months of your living expenses. In addition, you want to set aside enough money in this bucket for known major purchases or expenses in the next three to five years—a new roof, for example, or a car or a family cruise.

Emergency fund

***Known purchases/ expenses within the next 5 years**

***Liquid**

The investments in this bucket will primarily be bank products, because the purpose is to keep it safe and to be able to get to it quickly. If your car breaks down, you will want a source of readily available money to fix or replace it. You wouldn't want to have to sell any investments for an expense like that. If you were to put these funds at risk, hoping for growth, some of it could lose value instead. You don't need that worry. The money in this bucket may not be earning much, but that is not the goal here. The whole point is that it needs to be there for you when you need it.

This takes careful planning because you do not want to set aside too much money this way. You need to figure out the appropriate amount for potential emergencies and near-term anticipated expenses (within three to five years). You want sufficient cash at hand—but not too much. *Fully fund your emergency fund, but don't overfund it* so that you don't lose value due to inflation. By utilizing all three buckets, you will have more freedom to do this.

THE INCOME BUCKET

The income bucket contains the assets required to produce your desired lifetime income. It can cover both your living expenses and your lifestyle expenses (your needs and your wants). You might think of this as the bucket that represents what retirement looks like to you.

The money in this account will not be liquid. It must stay in place so that it can produce the necessary cash flow. To find out how much you need in this bucket, you first need to calculate your personal-income need, then subtract your other guaranteed-income sources, such as Social Security benefits and pension payments. The difference is what this bucket will need to produce. That is the gap you need to fill. A very important part of the planning process is determining your income gap—the difference between your income goal and your guaranteed income sources.

Income

Determine income need:
- living expenses
-lifestyle expenses

Subtract guaranteed income sources

Solve for the gap

Use the least amount of assets to guarantee the level of income that you want

*Not-liquid

Your goal should be to use the least amount of assets necessary to guarantee your desired level of income. That is why I tend to recommend annuities for this bucket. You want to use as little as possible to get to your target income, leaving as much of your resources as possible for other uses, i.e., your growth bucket.

Determine the Gap

First determine if you have enough guaranteed income to cover your Living Expenses. This is a priority for many retirees.

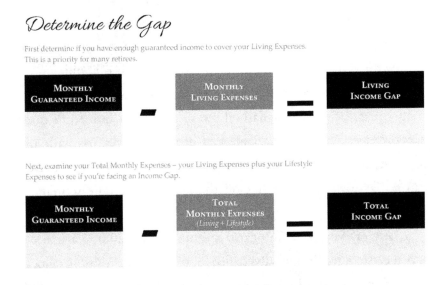

Next, examine your Total Monthly Expenses – your Living Expenses plus your Lifestyle Expenses to see if you're facing an Income Gap.

ANNUITIES FOR INCOME

There are two primary reasons why I believe that the best way to fund your income bucket is with an annuity. First, an annuity can usually provide the same income stream for less money than any other traditional method. If you were to choose stocks or bonds to produce the same income, it would require more assets. Next, an annuity can eliminate the risk of outliving your assets because it provides an income stream that you cannot outlive. Therefore, this product can eliminate two of the biggest risks to your retirement income: longevity risk and sequence-of-returns risk. It is the only product that guarantees lifetime income, which is why some advisors have labeled it as "sleep insurance."

I don't generally recommend an annuity as a growth vehicle but rather for income generation. It is designed to create a guaranteed income stream that you can't outlive. It's like buying your own personal pension. In short, the proper annuity is less risky, guarantees lifetime income, and delivers more "bang for the buck" compared to any other income-producing strategy. In doing so, it frees up more money for you to use in your growth bucket, which is liquid.

That is not to say that all annuities are equal. Some can be inappropriate and risky, particularly if put to the wrong use. Some carry excessive fees. Some are variable and others are fixed. As with any investment, you must choose wisely. In general, however, annuities can go far toward taking risk off the table for a secure retirement income.

Let's say you have $800,000 and will need $20,000 a year for income. In a traditional diversified portfolio with a 60/40 allocation of equities and bonds, you would need to set aside $500,000 and make withdrawals at the standard and supposedly safe rate of 4 percent annually to get your $20,000 a year. After setting aside that $500,000, you would have $300,000 left in your growth bucket. Alternatively, you could buy an annuity for $400,000 and get a guaranteed 5 percent, producing the same $20,000 a year. However, now you have $400,000 remaining in your growth bucket.

That means that for a smaller investment, you have a more secure income with much less risk, and you now have an additional $100,000 that can be liquid and allocated toward growth. What can you do with it? You could put it in your growth bucket as a long-term investment for future use or have fun with it or provide a legacy for your heirs with it. You have created that opportunity.

Most people caution that you should be safe with all your money in retirement. That need not be the case. You do need to have some liquid money and enough money to produce sufficient income, but then you can be as aggressive as you wish with the rest—and in this case, you have just boosted that potential considerably. You can afford to put that money at risk in hope of better returns. And you can do that without worrying about whether you will be able to pay the bills.

Of course, an annuity is only as strong as the insurance company that is backing it up, so be sure to review the ratings, safety, and reliability of the underlying insurance company before you purchase an annuity. But if you take the right actions to protect your income assets, you should be free of worry, all the way through your retirement, about whether you will have enough income. When you are eighty years old, you don't want to fret about how the market might be diminishing your future income stream.

THE GROWTH BUCKET

In your growth bucket, you will invest money that you have designated for future income needs as well as future purchases and expenses. This is your long-term bucket that will help to offset the potential of a future "HIT" that you could take from health-care expenses, inflation, and taxes.

Your aim here will be to determine the rate of return required to meet your long-term goals and then choose market investments to accomplish them. You will need the appropriate asset allocation and diversification—taking the least amount of risk for the desired results.

Because this will be money that you may be putting at risk in hopes of a greater return, this bucket must have a time horizon of five years or longer. These assets generally will be liquid. As time goes by, and this bucket fills up sufficiently, you will be able to take money out of it to increase your income level if necessary. In other words, the purpose of this money is to refill or resupply the other buckets as necessary.

Growth

Determine rate of return for need/goal

Take the least amount of risk for the desired result

Choose asset allocation

Diversity

Investment/portfolio selection

*Liquid

Let's say you create a plan and follow it exactly. You have your bank accounts for emergencies and known purchases or expenses in the next five years. You have money set aside in annuities, safe from market risk, to produce the amount of income that you want. Your remaining assets are placed in a diversified portfolio so that the only funds you have at risk are in this growth bucket, which you do not foresee using for at least five years. This allows you to capitalize on *the power of time, which is perhaps the most important aspect of successful stock market investing.*

Now what if the market slumps this month or next year? If it does, your spirits won't be slumping with it. You can continue to enjoy retirement without having to cut back on your plans for the next five years. *Your income will be secure, your emergency fund will be in place, and your growth portfolio will have the time that it needs to recover.* You can leave it alone. You won't be panicking. The market will have years to cycle back upward. With your five-year plan firmly in place, you will know that you can still buy that car or take that trip, even if your growth portfolio is down 10 percent. That is the peace of mind that you deserve at this stage of your life.

EVERYTHING IN ITS PROPER PLACE

Each of your portfolio buckets should be a separate account. The biggest mistake people make is trying to accomplish those differing purposes within a single portfolio. It is too risky to try to address your liquidity, income, and growth needs all in the same bucket.

That is the problem with the typical risk-assessment questionnaires used in the financial industry. Those questions are appropriate only for the assets in your growth bucket, because all the rest of your money should already be set aside and safe. If you are using my three-bucket approach, you undoubtedly would answer such a questionnaire differently than if you kept all your money together.

If you have a total portfolio of $800,000, for example, but you know that the questionnaire only applies to the $400,000 that you have allocated for growth, you will answer those questions differently because you know you can invest it more aggressively. Why not? Since your income and liquid assets are safe. You will be investing from a position of confidence, knowing that your growth money will have time to recover if the market falters. However, if you think the questionnaire applies to all of your life savings, you must confront those old worries about running out of money. You will be investing from a position of fear, and you may become too conservative with all your assets.

A "one-size-fits-all" portfolio is likely to allocate your retirement assets ineffectively. For example, you may be tying up more of your assets than necessary to generate income. The result is that you lock up too much of your money without recognizing how some of it might be put to better use to meet your needs and goals.

Consider the account that you earmark to produce income as not being liquid, even if the investments you are using to produce your income technically are. Whether your income will come from an annuity, dividends, bond interest, or something else, you should refuse to dip into that source for any other reason. Consider it untouchable except for the income stream that it produces. You need to keep that account intact, so that it will keep generating your retirement paycheck. For all practical purposes, assume that those assets don't exist.

Therefore, if you need $20,000 to buy a car, you will go to your growth bucket for that money, not to your income bucket. If you do the latter, you will have less money coming in next year. That is not the direction you want to go.

Out there in the marketplace of finances, you will find "annuity people" and "stock-picking people" and folks who just want to sell you insurance. Many advisors do have a specific point of view. To me, it depends on your purpose for the money. An annuity may not be a good fit for your liquid bucket, but it could work very well for your income bucket and, depending on your risk tolerance level, may or may not work for some portion of your growth bucket. A mutual fund portfolio may be a great fit for your growth bucket but not for your income bucket, etc.

You can easily find radio shows and seminars where the sole focus is on annuities. The message is that everyone needs to own annuities, regardless of their needs or goals. I regret that some in our industry put such misinformation out there. I'm not an "annuity guy," nor am I a "market guy" or an "insurance guy." What I am is a "protect-your-lifetime-income guy." I am in favor of all of those if they are in the right bucket and serving the right purposes for your retirement. I am against all of those if they are used improperly. They need to be a good fit.

The three-bucket approach represents the philosophy behind so much of what you have been reading in the preceding chapters. This is the practical application to help you produce the peace of mind to move you toward a happy retirement. We have talked about many risks that are critical to address in your retirement years—longevity, inflation, taxes, long-term care, sequence of returns, and others. Now you can see just where and how, in your overall plan, you will deal with each of these risks.

Your retirement is too important to relegate it to a guessing game of a little here, a little there. With the three-bucket approach, you can have confidence that your goals are being met, your assets are properly allocated, and you have a plan—a plan that will allow you to have peace of mind while at the same time affording you the freedom to enjoy life.

That is the key to *simplifying your retirement.*

CHAPTER 8

The Wise Advisor

In my first job in the financial industry, when I worked for an insurance company, it didn't much matter what people told me about their situation. What I concluded was that they needed insurance. That was my training, that was my job, and frankly that was all that I was licensed to do. My business card, though, generously identified me as a "financial representative," seeming to suggest that I was qualified to offer an array of services.

In my second job, at a broker-dealer, my business card called me a "financial advisor." By that, clients might have assumed that they were getting unbiased advice without conflict of interest. The truth was that mutual-fund representatives would take us out to lunch, and the firm sold proprietary products. Our research team would tell us which stocks and funds should be our focus. In that job, there was not as much selling of insurance products.

All along the way, though, I felt called to be a fiduciary, even when it was not required of me. I wanted to act in the client's best interest because it was the right thing to do. In my previous roles, my responsibility was to only recommend what was suitable for clients—which can be much different from what is in their best interest. If a mutual fund could serve their purposes, for example, we could put them in one with higher fees or that paid higher commissions.

It is little wonder that many people just do not know whom to trust. Many times, a financial advisor is a "captive agent" who can only sell insurance or only sell investment products. It seems that anyone who works for a year or so in the financial industry nowadays also gets "vice president" printed on his or her business cards. Don't be fooled by titles given out by financial companies or brokerage firms. How do you find someone you can count on? You need an advisor who is *independent*, which means the firm they represent is not owned by any investment or insurance companies, does not have proprietary products, and has no incentives to offer one product over another.

Typically, independent advisors are *fee-based*. Depending upon what is appropriate, they can recommend an insurance product or an investment portfolio. They have no conflict of interest. Such an advisor may get paid a commission for selling an insurance product or they may charge an investment management fee for managing the assets. In any case, you will know what you are getting, why you are getting it, and what you are paying for it.

You also should be looking for an advisor who is *full-service*. He or she can talk to you about insurance products or about investment products. A full-service advisor is knowledgeable about both, looks at your situation from every angle for the best fit, and makes recommendations based on your needs and goals. You can learn objectively about the benefits and limitations of both approaches.

Certainly, the news is full of stories that make people wary. We hear of rip-offs such as the Bernie Madoff scam. We learn of the role that the financial industry played in the housing-market crisis. A major brokerage firm recently faced a huge fine because more than five thousand advisors had collected a fortune in fees since 2011 by opening millions of customer accounts without their knowledge. Things like that breed widespread skepticism—and the suspicions run even deeper when you add such popular recent movies as *The Wolf of Wall Street* and *The Big Short*. Often, when people walk through my office door, they are not quite sure what I'm all about or exactly how to know whom they should trust.

The financial planning firm that I started over ten years ago is a registered investment advisor firm. This type of structure means that I am obligated to adhere to a much higher standard than is typical for the financial industry—simply put I must act as a *fiduciary* for my clients. When I explain that it means the law requires us to *do what is in the client's best interest*, they often seem puzzled as if wondering, "Isn't that the case for everybody in the industry?" No, it's a much higher standard than what has long been typical—although new Department of Labor rules are narrowing that gap.

My firm makes use of *third-party custodians*, which have custody of clients' assets and issue statements telling them exactly how much is in their accounts and how it is invested. You never want your financial advisor to custody your assets or produce statements. That opens the door to Ponzi schemes and other abuses that hit the headlines. You need the objectivity and validity of a trusted third-party custodian (e.g., our firm uses Charles Schwab).

It's also important to understand the meaning of all those letters you see after an advisor's name. If possible, seek out someone who is a CERTIFIED FINANCIAL PLANNER™ practitioner, or CFP® professional. The CFP® certification represents a high level of competency, ethics, and professionalism. And since a CFP® professional is also held to a fiduciary standard, they are required to act in your best interest. And there are a variety of other credentials that designate areas of specialty and accomplishment as well.

It's not hard, with a little online research, to learn the meaning of all that alphabet soup. Just be aware that the terms "financial advisor" or "financial representative" don't tell you much. Almost anybody can hang that shingle. Those words on my business cards in my early career did not make me a financial planner. It was not my job to listen carefully and find out what people really needed so that I could determine which options would be right for them. My job was to make the sale. If someone walked in with $100,000 to invest, I would have had some product ready to go soon after the handshake. I was simply a salesman.

That didn't sit right with me. I wanted to truly help people. I wanted to help them change their lives and find peace of mind. Those early experiences were valuable for me, in that I learned a lot and they helped me support my young family, but I wanted something more—and I wanted something more for my clients, as well. I knew there must be a better way. That is what led me to eventually start my own business—an independent, full-service, fee-based, fiduciary investment advisor firm—and what compelled me to fulfill the requirements to become a CERTIFIED FINANCIAL PLANNER™ practitioner. I was determined to take the time with my clients to get it right and custom-design financial plans just for them.

ADVICE IN ALL THE WRONG PLACES

People get inappropriate advice from lots of places, and Wall Street is one of them. My focus is Main Street, not Wall Street. I help people grow their resources, and I only do well when they do well. The focus

of Wall Street is buying and selling. Stockbrokers make their commissions when securities are on the move and their clients are getting
in and out of investments.

Wall Street has a vested interest in motivating investors to act by
appealing to the human emotions of greed and fear. The prevailing
message is: "Don't just stand there, do something." In other words:
"Generate commissions for us." The middleman takes a cut, too.
With every buy and sell, there's a markup on the stock-market floor.
If you buy a stock and sell it even a second later, you will not get the
same price.

The incentives are simply not in place on Wall Street to encourage
people to invest prudently. Brokers are counting on a certain lack of
discipline and a prevailing daily anxiety so that investors react with
every rise and fall of the market: "It's time to sell! It's time to buy!
Don't lose! Don't lose out!" That's the message by which Wall Street
wins. The brokers need you to "do something" so that they can make
their money.

To further confuse matters, some of the big Wall Street firms
have close ties to the media outlets. They have an ownership interest
in financial magazines, for example. They also advertise heavily, which
can give them an edge in the content. When you see words such as
"The five funds you must own this year" emblazoned on the glossy
cover, you cannot be sure that the information is unbiased. Financial
media can present a lot of good advice on personal finances—how
to save money on your electric bill, for example, or the best time to
buy airline tickets, and many other consumer tips and tools. That's
all valuable for general readership. What can hurt you is paying
attention to those articles that try to tell you which securities you
need right now or who's hot and who's not among money managers
You should not take your financial advice from a magazine or some

radio or television host. It is generic information that may work for some situations but certainly not in every situation.

In this book, we have already looked at the wide range of factors that go into financial decision-making. How old are you? For what do you intend to use the investment—for income, emergencies, legacy, to offset taxes and inflation? The Wall Street media are interested in the masses, not the individual. Those talking heads cannot look you in the eye. The media commentators do not know you. The newsletter writers and stock-picking scribes have never shaken your hand or asked how your family is doing. Sound advice arises from a relationship.

Having a subscription might make you feel as if you have an edge up with the so-called experts—as if you are on an inside track to riches—but that does not mean that they are right. Instead, you could end up doing something that is very wrong for you. In many cases, the pundits are appealing to fear and greed. They urge you to follow the crowd while you can. That is their version of wisdom. It is a financial given, however, that it is risky to choose investments based upon past performance. Those top-ten lists are ever changing. This year's list does not resemble last year's. The bright stars tend to blink out, even as new ones are rising.

Good advice for your neighbor could very well be poor advice for you. Every investment has a place. It just needs to serve a specific purpose. A bad investment could very well be one that is just in the wrong place. It's a bad fit. Is gold always bad? No. Is gold right for everybody? No. It depends. With any financial product, the biggest variable is you. Does it meet the need that you are trying to fulfill? Are you trying to pay for your children's college education, or are you arranging for retirement income? The circumstances govern the choices. You should not base your investment decisions on somebody else's preferences.

Your coworkers will have plenty to say in the lounge and on social media. You will hear about their big winners. They will prescribe the surefire best way to pick the bulls from your 401(k)-investment menu. You may be in a different place in life. Your coworker—or your brother-in-law, or uncle, or backyard buddy—does not share your circumstances. Again, what is fitting for them may not fit you. Their goals are not your goals. And besides, you only hear about the home runs. They don't announce at the water cooler when they took a big loss. You need to do what is right for you, without apologies. It's *your* life and *your* peace of mind.

THE ROI OF A GOOD ADVISOR

If you listen to any advice from your friends and colleagues, perhaps it would be finding out who is doing a good job as their financial advisor. Find out whether that advisor serves people who have something in common with your stage of life. Some people balk at the thought of paying anything—whether a commission or a fee—to an advisor and instead decide they will try to handle it all themselves. I understand that motivation, but I would point them to a study by DALBAR, an independent research firm in Boston, that analyzes individual investor portfolios and compares their performance with major stock-market indices over a twenty-year period. Invariably, the DIY investors always underperform. By saving the expense of the fee, it costs them more in the returns.

Why is that? Individual investors tend to move money a lot more. They get in and out of investments. They buy and sell. Over time, that erodes the return. They think they're going to save the cost of having to pay a fee to a qualified advisor—and by that I do not mean a stockbroker, who is part of the problem, but rather a fiduciary advisor who is solidly on their side. They figure they can find out whatever they need to know, and besides, they tell themselves, they have these three subscription newsletters giving them an inside track.

Tragically, over time they slip behind, despite what they save on fees and perhaps on transaction costs. The root of the problem is that they generally are not as strong emotionally and rationally as they imagine themselves to be. They cannot stand firm in their convictions in the face of market fluctuations that bring out the human emotions of fear and greed. As a result, they make mistakes in their investment choices and timing, and their returns suffer. It is difficult to stay disciplined and prudent without a committed financial advisor by your side.

A study by Vanguard quantified the value of a financial advisor. The study concluded that an advisor who helps clients to build diversified portfolios and invest in a disciplined manner is worth about 3 percent a year. That is an impressive statistic—and it came from a company that encourages self-investing. The study indicates that it costs significantly more to do it on your own than to pay the right type of advisor and planner to help you. It might seem that you can save money, but the historical data proves that a good advisor actually adds value to the portfolio rather than subtracts from it. The advisor's fee more than pays for itself.

You want an advisor who will give you customized advice, educate you on the right choices, and encourage you to stick with your plan while others are insisting that you should react irrationally. A qualified advisor working on your behalf is worth real percentage points in your portfolio.

To manage a portfolio, my firm charges a flat fee of 1 percent or less of its total value. If we are utilizing a stock, bond, mutual fund, or exchange-traded fund portfolio, we just charge the flat 1 percent fee based on the value of those accounts. This fee is paid directly from those accounts. If we recommend an insurance product or annuity—for which the insurance company pays us—we do not charge our clients on those assets.

An advisor who charges an investment advisory fee based on the value of your account has a vested interest in your portfolio. In other words, if the portfolio loses money, the advisor makes less. If the portfolio gains, the advisor earns more. Their objective is aligned with yours. There is no conflict of interest. Advisors who get a commission, however, lay claim to 5 or 6 percent or so up front—and however the recommended portfolio performs has no impact on that amount. When commission-based advisors suggest you switch to a different investment in the future, you understandably might wonder whether it's just to generate a paycheck for them.

Some people remain enamored at the thought of working with the huge financial firms, the big names that are widely recognized. Never mind the name on the building or the logo on the letterhead; you need a trusting relationship with the individual sitting down across the table from you—the person who will talk about what really matters in your life. By the way, a robo-advisor cannot do that for you.

All the best performers have a coach. Before I entered this industry, I was a coach. I helped young people discover how to reach their potential and to work cooperatively on a team. They came to appreciate the discipline necessary to accomplish goals. Coaching is in my nature—I encourage people to be their best, and I bring that strength to my profession.

At my firm Wise Wealth, LLC, our relationships are based on trust, not transactions. We look at you not as a customer but as a client. You are not just a consumer buying something. You deserve attentive service and continuing advice that adds increasing value through the years.

You need a plan that leads to financial peace of mind. Your plan needs to be constantly monitored to adapt to changes in health, goals, time frame, needs, etc.

WISE WEALTH PLANNING PROCESS

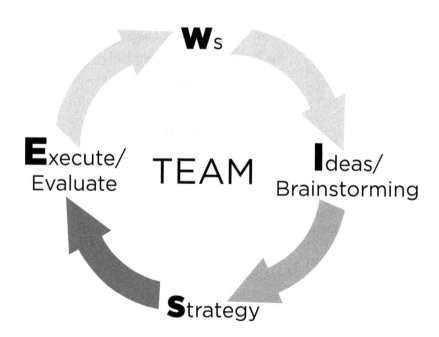

We have a clear process that we take every potential client through at Wise Wealth. To help them grasp the essentials of our approach to financial planning, I suggest that they think of the word "WISE" as an acronym:

- **W** is for the "who, what, when, where, why." This is what we are covering in our first meeting. I want to find out what my clients' vision and goals are for retirement, how much income they might need, what their legacy goals are, and how they acquired their current investments. We talk about our philosophy and approach, and we get to know each other. We will gather the information that will be critical in putting together a customized plan.

- **I** is for ideas. In our second meeting, we provide options on ways to accomplish the goals and objectives of the client and begin clarifying the plan. I am looking for feedback and confirmation that we are on the right track. Often, clients at this point will begin to refine their thoughts on what they want in retirement—how much income they expect, for example, or how much money they would like to leave to their children.

- **S** is for strategy. In our third meeting, we narrow down the strategy, based on the information and feedback of the first two sessions. We talk about specific steps that we will need to take in order to put the plan in place, such as how we will deal with their need for liquid money, income, and growth assets. It is at this point where I feel that it is appropriate to make specific investment recommendations. We would also discuss the process of opening accounts and transferring assets.

- **E** is for execute and evaluate. Having developed the plan, we then get together to put the plan in place and then regularly monitor it. Those review meetings can be semiannual or annual, depending on circumstances. We make changes as necessary to stay with the plan. You need to be comfortable with change, because it is inevitable. We may need to adjust course over time, just as anyone driving a car or piloting a plane must do to reach a destination.

It's not enough to have a plan in your pocket. You must implement it and use it. Once you make the decision to choose Wise Wealth as your partner, the value is just beginning. We work together to manage your money with wisdom. We consult, explain, and educate. What is more important than buying investments is buying into the plan—because that is the wellspring for financial peace.

In a decade, your needs and goals and time frame will likely not be the same as when we put your initial plan in place. Besides the regular reviews that we initiate, our clients are free to come to us with concerns and updates whenever they wish. We do not add any fees for that continuing service. We understand that circumstances change, however, the principles of sound planning do not.

A TEAM APPROACH

At Wise Wealth, we bring in experts on taxes, estate planning, long-term care, and other areas to speak to our clients, at no charge to them. We set up those opportunities for our clients to get the knowledge and help they need. It is part of what makes our relationship much more than transactional.

I often refer people to lawyers and accountants and other specialists. I believe in a strong network. I identify professionals who share my company's values and approach. They understand the importance of consulting and educating. Your estate-planning attorney, for example, should have a wider vision than just advocating that everyone needs a trust. I want everyone in the network to truly listen to your needs and to be concerned about you for the long term. That is what you should expect of me. Expect it of others as well.

I am happy to attend those meetings with your other professionals to provide perspective and information, with your approval. If you already have your own attorney and others with whom you have been working, we will work with them; otherwise, we can refer you to the experts in our network. I help to coordinate the members of the team and complement their work. After a meeting with an estate-planning attorney, for instance, we often assist clients with a lot of changes, such as putting together a trust and updating accounts, titling, and beneficiaries. By bringing us all together as a team, you gain a better view of your overall financial picture.

As a CFP° professional, I have the wide range of knowledge to offer advice on taxes and estate planning. My company does not do the actual work of preparing tax returns or drawing up wills or trusts, but we do examine your overall tax and estate situation and make recommendations such as which accounts would be best for retirement income and which might serve better to leave to your heirs. Our approach is holistic; we keep track of the whole picture.

The law requires me to act in people's best interest, but I abide by an even deeper ethic, often called the "golden rule." Not only do I carry out my fiduciary responsibility, but I take to heart the guiding biblical principle from Matthew 7:12: *So in everything, do to others what you would have them do to you.*

CHAPTER 9

A Legacy beyond Wealth

"What is most important to you?" I always ask individuals and couples when designing a financial plan. "Do you want to maximize the use of your money while you are alive, or are you hoping to leave behind as much as you can?"

Those in the generation now planning for retirement will generally tell me that they want to get the most use of their money during their lifetime. Couples tell me that their kids can have whatever is left—because, after all, they have spent enough on them already.

It's not that people care less these days about what they leave behind. Although they may not be thinking of a specific sum to leave to those in the next generation, they are still quite interested in their welfare. Many times they are thinking of something else they want to leave behind. They want to bestow a legacy of more than just money.

GROWING ASSETS FOR POSTERITY

Of the three buckets in your financial plan—the liquid, income, and growth buckets that we examined in chapter 7—the latter is the one that will deliver the resources for your legacy. When considering how much you will leave behind, the focus will not be on your liquid money or on spending money in your income stream. Legacy planning is a primary role of the growth bucket.

For that reason, I need to discover early in the planning process the extent to which you desire to leave resources to family or charity. Do you have a dollar amount in mind that is your goal for each child, or grandchild, or the causes and institutions that are meaningful to you? Is there anyone in the family who needs special support? Or do you want to elevate your lifestyle during your retirement years, earmarking the remainder for those heirs?

This discussion is just as important as the others that we will have early in our financial-planning relationship. Just as we will have in-depth discussions about your liquidity needs and your income needs, we must also get clear about your legacy aspirations. I need to know what you want to do so that together we can design a growth bucket that can make it happen.

As I have emphasized in discussing other aspects of financial planning, it is too late to make a mistake at this stage of life. This holds true for legacy planning as well. We need to make sure that you are investing in the most appropriate manner so that your growth bucket will be able to meet all the demands that are placed upon it. As you will recall, this is also the bucket that protects you from taking a HIT from health-care expenses, inflation, and taxes. So, if you wish to provide significant legacy resources as well, your growth bucket must be big enough and invested purposefully enough to accommodate that noble goal.

When I hear couples say that they have no specific amount in mind for their legacy ("The kids can just have the house and whatever's left when we're done.") they are communicating to me that they do not have any great need for legacy-planning tools in their growth bucket. These are often couples who have launched their children into successful careers of their own and who now want to enjoy their savings for themselves.

Other times, I will hear comments such as, "We have decided that each of our three children should get $300,000 after we have passed away." Not only is the intention clear but so is the amount. In such cases, we can start investigating how to best use proceeds from the growth bucket to accomplish those objectives.

Often, the solution involves insurance planning. What would it cost, for example, for a couple to purchase a guaranteed universal life insurance policy, with the emphasis on the death benefit rather than the cash value? Paying for the insurance can be a lot less expensive than trying to leave the equivalent amount of money behind through the return on investments—not to mention that with life insurance there is a guaranteed payout and death benefit proceeds are tax-free. It is an efficient way to plan, particularly when we know the dollar amount. We can find out how much insurance and how big a premium is required to meet that objective.

Once that portion is guaranteed for legacy purposes, then we can know what other assets in the growth bucket are available for use during retirement. With this strategy, you gain clarity. Otherwise, you would wonder how much money you can spend and still meet your legacy goals. You could find yourself once again worrying about the unknowns. You would not know whether you were overspending or unnecessarily scrimping.

There is no right or wrong answer. Some people want to spend every penny of their life savings by the day they die. They want to arrange their finances to accomplish their goals while still having enough money to last throughout their lifetime. Some people want to set up their children to elevate their lifestyle or to leave a specific sum to help pay for each of the grandchildren's college expenses.

It comes down to your end-of-life wishes. If they are to come true, then you must plan for them. Whether your desire is to leave a legacy or not—and you may have good reasons either way—you need to know what demands will be placed upon the investments that you are setting aside for the future. Then we can choose the products that are the most cost-effective and best-suited for accomplishing whatever legacy goals you might have in mind.

EQUALIZING THE ESTATE

Some couples, especially if they have been running a business, are concerned about "equalizing" the estate—in other words, leaving a legacy that is fair to each of the children. For example, let's say that you are a plumber but that only one of your three sons has learned the trade and aspires to take over your business. What about the other two? One is a carpenter, and one is an accountant. Do they deserve nothing simply because they chose other careers? They might not be interested in how to run pipes, but you can be sure that they are very interested in what becomes of the family wealth.

Most families want to equal out the inheritances. The tool by which this can be accomplished most effectively is life insurance. The plumber son gets the business. The other sons get an insurance payout in the amount that represents the value that each would have received for a third of the shares of the business. The family works out the details in advance—who will get what and how much of it, when, and why—through careful estate- and business-transfer planning.

Leaving a business equally to all the children, some of whom couldn't care less about it, is a design for disaster. Leaving it all to the only child who is interested, however, could foster resentment and feelings of favoritism. Such a strategy could splinter family relationships for generations.

A survivorship life insurance policy that pays out after both mom and dad are gone can prevent such unfortunate consequences. Many families have found it to be the optimal solution—again, because the money is guaranteed and goes to the heirs free of taxes. We find it to be the least expensive way to accomplish these goals and keep everybody happy.

BASIC DOCUMENTS OF ESTATE PLANNING

As we discuss legacy matters, let's look at some of the basic documents that will likely be included in your estate planning. Every family should have these. The only exception is the trust—but I include it here because for many families it is a valuable means to control and protect assets while potentially reaping significant tax benefits. To get all these documents in order, I refer my clients to attorneys who specialize in them. These are legal papers that need to be drafted with precise language by an experienced and qualified professional.

WILL

This is the fundamental means by which you can pass on your resources to the next generation or to other heirs or charities. If you have minor children, the will is also how you can name a guardian for them. In your will, you designate an executor who will file the document in probate court upon your death. That person is responsible for working with the court to distribute your assets in the way that you have specified and to make sure that final taxes, expenses, and debts have been paid. The proceedings of probate court are open to the public, which you should keep in mind if privacy is a concern.

REVOCABLE LIVING TRUST

Because the will has no bearing until the time of death, you may wish to do other estate planning to take care of your assets if you are unable to do so while you are alive. A revocable trust provides for managing your financial affairs while you are alive, even if you are incapacitated, and its provisions continue after you die. You can put stipulations on distribution of assets, and a properly structured trust can provide protection from creditors and lawsuits. The terms of the trust dictate how assets will be distributed. In fact, those provisions can extend your influence for generations to come. Prior to death, those terms and provisions can be changed at any time. If you act as your own trustee, you can continue to manage your own financial affairs and investments.

DURABLE POWER OF ATTORNEY

Who will act on your behalf if you cannot? A durable power of attorney (POA) is a document that authorizes someone of your choosing to take those actions. That person will generally be given the discretion to invest or spend your assets, although you can set up the document to limit those powers. The POA is called durable because it endures through the time that you are unable to make your own decisions and take your own actions. It does not continue after your death, however.

HEALTH-CARE POWER OF ATTORNEY

If you cannot make your own medical decisions, this document names someone whom you wish to give that power. It is separate from the other durable power of attorney and specifically addresses medical issues. Disagreements over the best course of medical care for a loved one can divide families, and sometimes such matters end up in court. You can avoid that kind of conflict by legally appointing the one who can decide on your behalf. That way there will be no question about who has the authority.

ADVANCE MEDICAL DIRECTIVE

Should doctors take measures to sustain your life if you are on life support or permanently unconscious and you are unable to tell them how you feel about that? You can make sure they know your desires for end-of-life care by filing with them, and with the hospital, an advance medical directive, which often has been called a "living will." It makes your desires known and helps to release the doctors from liability when they follow your directive. A living will, however, doesn't give another person the right to speak on your behalf. That is why you need the health-care power of attorney as well.

BENEFICIARY DESIGNATIONS

In working with our clients on their estate planning, we take a close look at whom they have designated as beneficiaries on any of their assets that will be passed on by contract. In other words, who is in line to inherit the 401(k), IRA investments, or the annuity? Who is listed as the recipient of the insurance payout? We make sure that those designations are correct.

Those beneficiary designations are extremely important because whoever's name is listed will get the money, no matter what a will or a trust says. That is why you should put a priority on making sure that the designations are accurate and that they accomplish your wishes. You can update them whenever necessary.

There have been situations where beneficiaries have not been updated and an ex-spouse was in line to receive all the money. As you can imagine, that could be a nightmare, and that is why you should examine who is listed on old 401(k)s and insurance policies and other contracts. Retirement plan administrators and insurance companies will give the proceeds to whoever is named on the form, and once you have passed away, the courts have little recourse but to honor your stated wishes—even if you have remarried.

Updating your beneficiaries is a simple matter. It costs nothing, but if you don't do it, the consequences could be severe. Sometimes, young people list a parent as beneficiary and don't change it to their spouse when they marry. Depending upon the quality of their relationship, the parent might be more than happy to accept the money!

Sometimes a parent will list the oldest child as beneficiary, assuming that he or she will distribute the money fairly among the siblings. This may or may not happen. Despite any informal agreement, the beneficiary has no legal obligation to share with anyone else. All the children need to be listed as contingent beneficiaries if you hope to ensure that they each will get his or her portion of the estate. Or if you have set up a trust, you can list the trust as beneficiary and then the proceeds will be dictated by the wishes you have laid out in your trust. So it's also important to keep your trust updated as well.

WILLS AND TRUSTS

After examining your beneficiary designations, you should look at any of your assets that will not pass by contract (i.e., via direct beneficiary designations such as TOD, POD, or stated in retirement accounts and insurance policies). You need to make sure that you have appropriately set up a will to direct the distribution of all your other possessions to your children and other heirs. Depending on your needs and wishes, you may also wish to establish a trust.

Because trusts have been a primary vehicle by which families manage estate taxes, some people falsely assume that they would only need a trust if the value of their estate were greater than the federal estate- and gift-tax exemptions. As of 2017, the exemption was set at $5.49 million per person, meaning that a couple with an estate of almost $11 million could leave that much to their heirs without paying any federal estate or gift tax. They would be taxed at the federal level only on the estate value above that amount. Many states observe those same exemptions but some tax at a much lower threshold.

The federal exemption in recent years has been much higher than it once was, but affluent families still feel the weight of that tax. Some estates can easily exceed $11 million—and the heirs can end up losing about half of any amount above that figure. In general, the higher exemption has helped many families pass on a financial legacy without having estate taxes become a huge issue.

Taxes, however, are just one thing you might wish to control after you are gone. Trust provisions can specify exactly who will get what and restrict how the recipients spend it. For example, a properly designed trust can be designated as your beneficiary. That way, your 401(k) or insurance proceeds will land in the trust upon your passing, instead of going directly to your children or other heirs.

Once the assets are in the trust, its carefully worded provisions can then put restrictions on how your money is distributed and used. Perhaps you do not want the kids to have all the money at once but want to limit them to 5 or 10 percent per year. Maybe you want them to receive only the interest on the principal. You could even specify that the money is to be used only if they need it for educational expenses, or for a first-time home purchase, or to establish a business, etc.

In other words, if for whatever reason you want or need to establish any sort of controls, such as how your children or heirs will be able to spend or receive those assets, then you must set up a trust. Neither a will nor a beneficiary designation can provide that level of control. Sometimes people want a trust because they have a spendthrift child who they feel would mishandle their money once it reaches their hands. They may put special restrictions upon that recipient, perhaps allowing withdrawals only under the guidance and approval of someone else.

Another reason to set up a trust would be to arrange for the lifelong care of a special-needs child. The trust could stipulate how the money would be distributed for the child's care through the years, setting forth the conditions and purposes so that no one can take advantage of those funds.

Because I understand the needs and goals of my clients, I can play a valuable role in helping them to lay the groundwork for an attorney to draft the legal and technical aspects. I do not have a law degree, but I can have the kind of conversations with my clients that will help them see which provisions would serve them well in their specific circumstances. I can help them communicate their wishes to an attorney, who will refine the wording of the documents. He or she will know the specific legal phrasing required to accomplish those wishes.

Your goal in estate and legacy planning should be to attain peace of mind about the resources that you will leave behind. If you have done comprehensive planning, you have found peace regarding your income, spending, investments, and other aspects of your financial life. You know the goals that you are striving for while you are alive. Now, you are setting goals for how your life's work will continue to serve others once you are gone.

You already have an estate plan, whether you know it or not, even if you have never thought about these matters. Your money will not be buried with you, but it will go somewhere—and if you do not have a plan, you can be certain that the government will put one in place for you. It might not be the plan that you would have chosen, however, and you will no longer be able to establish the controls that your family might need.

THE LOVING THING TO DO

In the news, we regularly hear tales of celebrities who passed away without an estate plan in place. What results is often a legal case, played out in the courts for public consumption. Even for folks who are not in the limelight, the lack of a clear estate plan can lead to quite a mess. Dealing with these matters well in advance is the loving thing to do. You are demonstrating that you care by showing your family that you want the best for everyone, even when you will not be around to help.

As with all aspects of financial planning, both spouses should be involved in these conversations. Both need to be aware of what is happening, and what will happen, with the family finances. One of the advantages of establishing a trust is that you need to take an inventory of all your assets—your real estate, your vehicles, everything you possess. I have seen cases where a surviving spouse had no idea where the accounts were or what was in them. Was there any life insurance? Was money tucked away in a bank somewhere?

Conducting that inventory brings clarity to both spouses on the extent and nature of the assets, how they are titled, and how they should be distributed. Nobody wants to be grappling with such concerns during their time of grief. But many people, because of a lack of planning, must do just that. Even as they are mourning, they find themselves sorting through old files trying to track down the money. An inventory would have made it so much easier on them.

When you organize to that level, you are doing a kindness to the loved ones who may someday need that information after you have passed away. I have met with widows and other family members who have struggled with not knowing where everything was kept. They are not fully confident, for example, whether they have accounted for life insurance that their dad or their husband might have obtained, and the uncertainty troubles them. It is hard enough to suffer the loss of a loved one without having to spend hours on the phone or to dig laboriously through files and boxes in search of account records and phone numbers and passwords. To get organized and spare your family that painful task is a gesture of love.

With or without a trust, our clients can take advantage of an online "vault" for secure storage of their inventory and other financial documents and statements. This makes recordkeeping particularly convenient. Even if one of the spouses is not as much involved in the couple's financial affairs, he or she should know the location of the inventory document that lists all the account numbers and locations. It is even easier when accounts are jointly titled, since the surviving spouse then will not have to make countless phone calls trying to gain access to those accounts. That can be a daunting task for someone already feeling overwhelmed. Your financial advisor should obviously have all of that information, but I also recommend that a family member have access as well.

I have many clients who are widows, and they have found comfort in knowing that we have all the information and can take them through every step as they request beneficiary proceeds and perform other necessary tasks following the funeral. Providing a detailed summary list of accounts and other information helps to lessen the confusion down the road. It amounts to a snapshot of the couple's financial life, easily updated for quick reference. That way the surviving spouse won't be saying someday, "I didn't know that he put $10,000 in that bank," or "I wonder when he bought that policy."

A surviving spouse should never feel pressured to make immediate decisions or become an on-the-spot expert. Learning to take over an unfamiliar responsibility can be an intimidating situation, and quick decisions made under those conditions are likely to turn out badly. A trustworthy advisor can help the surviving spouse move through the process slowly and help them feel comfortable about it. Good decisions at this point are crucial—and not all advisors offer the wisdom needed to make them.

Knowing that your loved ones will be in good hands will help to bring you financial peace. You are following through with a plan to do right by your family. You have cut through the details to define the outcome that matters most. It is all part of *simplifying your retirement.*

CHARITABLE GIVING

For many families, leaving a legacy has much to do with deciding which charities to support. What are the causes and institutions that have been most meaningful? When I ask people whether they would rather maximize their use of money during their lifetime or maximize what they leave behind, most will tell me that they have never thought much about it. If they do want to leave a legacy, though, they often would like to help charities as well as their children. They just do not know how to do so efficiently. Sometimes they think that it is a choice between one or the other—and that is not necessarily the case. A well-designed charitable plan can leave abundant resources to both, with only the tax collector cut out of the deal.

For assets that you are leaving by contract—your IRA, 401(k), life-insurance policy, or annuity—you can choose the percentages for each beneficiary. In other words, you could leave 10 percent to your church and the remaining 90 percent equally divided among your children. You can also list beneficiaries by percentage within a trust. It is another way that you can give back to your place of worship, your alma mater, or other charity.

You could also choose from various trusts designed for charitable giving. Households that have a potential estate tax liability, for example, have discovered that charitable remainder trusts or charitable lead trusts are extremely valuable. These tools can effectively lower your current tax liability or your future potential estate tax liability.

With a charitable-remainder trust, you can receive the interest from the value of your contribution during your lifetime, with the charity getting the remainder upon your passing. With the charitable-lead trust, you can set it up so that the charity gets the interest during the early years, and your family inherits what is left behind.

If you have a very large estate, you should consider one of these trusts whether you are charitably minded or not. Otherwise, your charity of choice will be the government, which will distribute your assets as it sees fit. Most people would rather choose their own charity so they have some control over who benefits. Again, if the estate value is greater than $5.49 million for an individual or almost $11 million for a married couple, anything above those numbers will be taxable.

That estate tax can be avoided through major charitable planning. There are a lot of tools that not only help affluent families save on their eventual estate tax and current income tax but that can also channel valuable resources toward good causes of their choosing. The use of a charitable trust can be particularly advantageous for owners of a closely held business who have most of their assets or net worth tied up in it. There are ways to transfer ownership into the charitable trust and avoid a lot of the tax on the gains of that business.

If you decide to leave a certain amount to charity, then the next step is to examine all your assets and determine which ones are fully taxable. Those are the ones that you should consider leaving to charities, because they receive your contributions free of taxes. A good choice would be the qualified money in your IRA or 401(k)-type account. If you were to leave that money to your children, taxes would have to be paid on the full amount. However, whatever you donate to a charity from a qualified account will not become taxable to your estate.

Meanwhile, you can most efficiently leave your children proceeds from a life-insurance policy, which are received income tax-free, and/or tax-free Roth IRA accounts. You could also leave nonqualified assets, which go to them free of tax, or for which they get a step up in basis—in other words, they inherit those assets based on their value at your death and are not responsible for paying tax on the capital gains from the time when you originally acquired the assets. It would make less sense to donate such assets to charity, which already have a tax advantage.

Many families also use a highly advantageous tool called a donor-advised fund for their charitable giving. There are many such funds. Personally, I use the National Christian Foundation, but almost every major brokerage firm also has a charitable fund, such as Fidelity Charitable or Schwab Charitable. Families can open an account and then name it. I call mine the Stricklin Family Giving Fund.

Whatever money or assets you place (donate) into your donor-advised fund is tax deductible in the year in which you make the contribution. However, the money can stay in the account and does not have go to a charity until a later date, which you choose. In other words, you get the tax deduction for the money on its way in, not on its way out of the fund—and the only place that it will be going when it comes out is to a qualified charity. Meanwhile, while the money remains in the fund, you can choose investment strategies and decide how to manage it so that it can efficiently grow over long periods of time.

Later, when you have a desire to give some of those resources to charity, you can distribute your donations from there. For example, if a hurricane strikes the coast, you might decide to make a special contribution. The money must go to a 501(c)3 or other nonprofit organization, such as a church or a mission. Different funds have different restrictions, so before opening one, you should find out its investment and distribution policies. You want to have as much freedom as you can get in deciding where your money will go.

Remember, this is a charitable donation, so once you place the money in the fund, you cannot get it back. What you gain is the flexibility to decide who will get which donations and when, and you can change your mind about supporting a charity if its mission ceases to please you. You can make your donations gradually, at your own pace. Sometimes people who sell a business or earn a major bonus during the year do not want to give the proceeds all at once to their church or charity. Instead, they can put the money in a donor-advised fund and then distribute it over time.

Often, families will build up their donor-advised fund and then give it to the children as an inheritance. The children are getting a pile of money that they must give away. They cannot cash it in. It can only go to charity. Imagine your kids inheriting some of your money that they get to use, but also inheriting this fund that requires them to get together and decide which charities they will support. It is a powerful way to build family unity. The family members must make joint decisions on what matters most to them. Those gatherings can become a legacy-planning event and a family tradition.

It is important for parents and children to get together in advance so that everyone knows how this will work. The message from the parents to the kids will go along these lines: "You're each going to get a fair share of our estate, but we want you all to know that we are putting 10 percent of the estate into our family donor-advised fund. Let me explain what that means. It means that money inside that fund can only be given to charity. So, once a year while I am alive, we are going to meet and determine as a family who we want to give this to. When I am gone, I expect you guys once a year to come together and do the same." Some families purchase life insurance so that the children can receive a tax-free death benefit that is equivalent to their share of the estate, and then they place the entire proceeds of the estate in their donor-advised fund. Depending on the size of the estate, you may want to consider using an irrevocable life insurance trust in conjunction with this strategy.

Donor-advised funds are a great way for families of modest means to set up their own inexpensive family foundation. For tax purposes, these funds simplify matters greatly because you don't have to file separate forms for a variety of charities that you support. You have just one for the donor-advised fund from which the money is distributed, and you have a convenient record of your charitable giving throughout the years. Some people do all their charitable giving through their donor-advised fund.

RESOURCES OF THE HEART

When people talk about what they want to pass on to the next generation, generally they are referring to money—but they often have in mind a lot more. They want to pass on the story of their life. They want to leave behind their wisdom to those who will follow. Along with the money, they want to leave a message. They are thinking in terms of their values, not just their valuables.

What have you found meaningful during your years on earth? What are the causes that you cherish? Which institutions do you admire? What does your family stand for? On what foundation did you build? This is the stuff of true legacy, and many family leaders place a high priority on what they can do for posterity. Many people in retirement devote themselves to charitable and volunteer work.

They want to demonstrate their dedication, and they want their loved ones to know what matters most to them.

I have often heard my mother and father talk about our family stories. They can tell them in detail, because they lived them, whereas I am sure that I could only relate parts of them. So often it is the case that the poignant details fade away as the decades pass. In many families, those stories get lost through the generations. The way to make sure that does not happen is to create a family history. Whether it is in print or audio or video, that record of triumphs and challenges will persist from parent to child to grandchild and beyond.

Your family history can trace the chronology of events and how the bonds of love grew through the years. It can include an appreciation of each of the children and grandchildren and your hopes for them. You can declare for all time what you believe to be important and eternal. If you are a person of faith, you can speak from your heart about your desire for the coming generations to discover for themselves what you know to be true. Imagine your descendants, long after your passing, watching that video and hearing your voice and seeing the sincerity in your eyes as you tell them about your faith, values, and dreams. What you are communicating could do far greater good than any amount of money that you might leave them.

In every chapter of this book, I have emphasized the theme of wisdom as the precursor of wealth. Wisdom guided you to financial success, and now you can pass on that wisdom to the coming generations. It will be the seed for their success as well. You are leaving behind more than household riches. These are the resources of your heart—a legacy beyond wealth.

CONCLUSION

True Riches

Many of the world's richest people have had relatively little money. Blessings come in many ways besides financial. I make my living by helping people plan their financial lives, but that goes far beyond money management and investing. The comprehensive approach that I advocate is about making the most out of life itself. What is your life all about? Once you know that, money becomes the servant and not the master.

Much of the financial industry, and many of those who call themselves advisors, put money first. Obviously, money is important—it's what makes things happen. It is the primary tool to accomplish your goals. But the first question you should be asking yourself is not "How much money can I make on my investments?" Instead, it should be "What kind of life do I want to live in retirement, and why?" In other words, *First wisdom; Then wealth.*

In your final days, as you look back over your years, will you be able to say that you have provided for your family well? What have you done for the benefit of those whom you will leave behind? If you keep your focus on such essential questions, the details will follow as you take your time to think it all through. You should make each decision within the greater context of a well-constructed plan.

A lot of people go through their lives without thinking very much about death. They keep busy, and life just happens to them. A much better approach is to have a plan. Throughout this book, I have pointed out the importance of financial peace of mind. Remember this: financial peace comes from having a plan for your life—which includes preparing for death with dignity. When it comes to peace of mind related to death, there is more at stake than just money. A sign that I read once said it very well: "Know Jesus know peace, No Jesus no peace." Dave Ramsey likes to say it this way, "...the only way to true financial peace is to walk daily with the Prince of Peace—Christ Jesus."

That is what I want for you. I want you to have peace of mind *to and through retirement* and as you breathe your last breath. I want you to know that you were a good steward of all that you were given and to know that you moved through life confidently in pursuit of your dreams. I want you to have planned the distribution of your assets wisely and efficiently while saving money on taxes and expenses. I want you to have the satisfaction of having pursued your dreams and fulfilled your purpose. I want you to know that you were diligent about protecting all those years of hard work and that you had a well-organized and purposeful financial plan for life.

Many years have passed now since my days in seminary and my early career, when I learned many truths about the financial industry. I felt restless then, wondering what God wanted for my life and how he intended to use me for his purposes. I discovered that he had a ministry in mind for me that was something other than full-time pastoral ministry. However, I am passionate and excited and fulfilled in my career and calling. I am doing what God created me to do—

helping lead others to the financial peace that will allow them to leave an enduring legacy.

I hope that you too will find peace and fulfillment along with joy and happiness as you plan for the best years of your life!

ABOUT THE AUTHOR

S tephen Stricklin is the president and founder of an independent, full-service wealth management firm. After starting his career as a teacher and a coach, Stephen took his passion of educating others and adapted it to the financial services industry. He was motivated by the desire to bring financial wisdom to his clients. He enjoys working with business owners, professionals, families, and individuals who believe that wealth is a tool that needs to be managed wisely in order to produce the best results.

After working as a representative of an insurance company and an advisor of a national investment brokerage firm, Stephen launched his own registered investment advisory firm, Wise Wealth LLC. The slogan he developed as he began remains the cornerstone of his firm and its advisors: First Wisdom, Then Wealth.

Stephen believes financial peace comes from having a plan, which is the basis for all other decisions. He is a CERTIFIED FINANCIAL PLANNER™ professional, a Certified Kingdom Advisor™ and he holds insurance and securities licenses. He believes in listening to his clients and creating customized financial plans based on their unique needs and goals.

More than being a fiduciary, Stephen and his team believe in the timeless principle known as the Golden Rule: treat others the way you would want to be treated. This philosophy sets Stephen and his team apart in a world of robo-advisors, online investing, and generic advice. He and his team of advisors seek to serve their clients' best interests and gauge their success only on if their clients feel successful. He provides financial education and motivation through his workplace financial education workshops and he provides financial inspiration and instruction to churches and faith-based organizations.

Stephen has been recognized as a finalist for Retirement Advisor of the Year by Retirement Advisor magazine, an annual honor bestowed on the top five retirement advisors in the nation. He also founded Simplify Your Retirement, a retirement-focused baby boomer course designed to empower pre-retirees and retirees to take control of their financial futures. He is an energetic and inspiring national public speaker and has been featured in Forbes, was quoted in U.S. News & World Report, has hosted his own radio show, and is a frequent TV guest.

Stephen is married to his wife Amy, and they have four children together. He resides in Lee's Summit, Missouri, where his firm is based. He enjoys traveling and spending time with his family and is an avid sports fan. He is active in his local church, sits on several non-profit boards, is involved in international missions, and is a significant contributor to many philanthropic endeavors.

For more information or to schedule Stephen Stricklin to speak at your event, please visit www.StephenStricklin.com.

Twitter: @Stricklin_S

LinkedIn: Stephen Stricklin

ABOUT OUR COMPANY

With its primary office located on Main Street in Lee's Summit, MO, Wise Wealth LLC is committed to working alongside you to build a solid financial future. We work with individuals and groups all across the country. Honesty, integrity, and the Golden Rule are at the core of how Wise Wealth operates. As an independent, full-service Registered Investment Advisor firm, Wise Wealth does not represent any particular third-party company or specific financial product and therefore acts solely in your best interest.

We proudly conform to the financial planning process and Code of Ethics as defined by the CFP Board of Standards and the Financial Planning Client Bill of Rights. We are an independent Registered Investment Advisor firm and member of the National Ethics Association.

We believe very strongly in helping people make informed financial decisions. We offer programs that both inform and provide planning strategies to meet a variety of needs.

- Wealth planning: to help you map your financial future.

- Wealth management: to provide you with investment strategies and solutions.

- Wealth transfer planning: to determine how and the most-efficient way to distribute your assets.

- Workplace financial education: to help employers provide "financial wellness" benefits to their employees.

- Financial ministries: Biblical financial management workshops for church groups and faith-based organizations.

Achieving and maintaining wealth requires the financial wisdom to make sound decisions instead of emotional ones. The Wise Wealth Planning Process allows us to learn about your long-term goals and dreams and then leverage our knowledge and experience to help you realize them.

Who, What, When, Where, Why
We not only ask, we listen carefully to your answers and then lay out your plan's foundation, based on your vision and values.

Ideas/Brainstorming
We discuss different ways to accomplish your plan.

Strategy
We provide specific strategies that best fit your plan.

Execute/Evaluate
We carry out your wishes and continually monitor your plan.

To engage with Stephen or one of his personally trained financial advisors who can take you through the process and help you develop your own customized retirement income plan, visit **www.wisewealth.com**. You can also find us on Facebook at "Wise Wealth, LLC."

ABOUT THE SIMPLIFY YOUR RETIREMENT COURSE

Simplify Your Retirement is an independent financial education company. The goal of the Simplify Your Retirement course is to take the complexity out of retirement planning and to provide main-street investors with peace of mind about retirement. Our goal is to empower baby boomers to prepare for a secure and peaceful retirement.

This course is a comprehensive personal finance course for those in the early stages of retirement or those about to retire. It addresses difficult retirement decisions such as income planning, Social Security maximization, and the risks to avoid. You'll learn how to incorporate health care, inflation, and their considerations into your overall plan. Upon completion, you'll be better prepared to take the necessary steps to create your own retirement strategy.

Courses are taught by licensed professionals who have been trained on the concepts in this book. To find out if a course is being offered in your area, go to **www.simplifyyourretirement.com.**